February 18, 2009

Dear Dave,

Pace bene! (peace and all good),
it is my great hope that some of
these words resonate and fill
you with joy.

Tom Beeman

Leading
from
Within

Leading
from
Within

Twelve Concepts for Leaders Who
Seek a Spiritual Frame of Reference

**Thomas E. Beeman
& Richard Glenn**

Providence House Publishers
PROVIDENCE PUBLISHING CORPORATION
FRANKLIN, TENNESSEE

Printed in the United States of America

09	08	07	06	05	1	2	3	4	5

Library of Congress Control Number: 2005934977

ISBN-13: 978-1-57736-352-1
ISBN-10: 1-57736-352-3

Cover design by Joey McNair

All Scripture quotations, unless otherwise noted, are taken from The Holy Bible, Douay Rheims Version, revised by Bishop Richard Challoner A.D. 1749–1752, 1899 Baltimore edition. First reprinted by TAN Books and Publishers, Inc., 1971.

Scripture quotations marked "RSV Catholic Edition" are taken from the Catholic Edition of the Revised Standard Version of the Bible, copyright 1965, 1966 by the Division of Christian Education of the National Council of the Churches of Christ in the United States of America. Used by permission. All rights reserved.

PROVIDENCE HOUSE PUBLISHERS
an imprint of
Providence Publishing Corporation
238 Seaboard Lane • Franklin, Tennessee 37067
www.providence-publishing.com
800-321-5692

*A man without . . . spiritual vision is like
a captain who finds himself in the midst
of an uncharted sea, without compass,
rudder and steering wheel.
He never knows where he is,
which way he is going,
and where he is going to land.*

WILLIAM J. H. BOETCKER

Contents

Preface

Concepts are ideas formed in the mind. They shape our thinking and often give us a plan or help us generate strategies to accomplish our goals. Without clear concepts we are at a great disadvantage. The entire design for our lives may be at risk if we cannot create some vision of what the future will be and, in turn, strategies that will help us make that future a reality. The following concepts help create a better future because they appeal to a spiritual vision. We believe this to be the compass and rudder for leaders who seek a frame of reference from above.

These concepts enhance leadership capacity by challenging our existing ideas with the intention of influencing leaders to cultivate virtue. If you were introduced to these concepts would you take advantage of them? Twelve such concepts are discussed here.

Leading from Within: Twelve Concepts for Leaders Who Seek a Spiritual Frame of Reference offers leaders the opportunity to explore thought-provoking and challenging ideas. Divided into sections—insight, awareness, decision making, and solitude—this book provides readers with a structure to reflect upon concepts related to those four particular dimensions in a leader's life.

While reading *Leading from Within* you will:

- Gain insight into yourself
- Seek to establish congruency between what you say and what you do
- Promote yourself in a way that inspires confidence in others
- Understand that one's viewing point may be more important than one's point of view
- Discover that the brain has two distinct strategies
- Gain perspective when feeling overwhelmed
- Learn to choose the results you want
- Discern when change is necessary
- Discover the necessity of spiritual friendships

- Listen to a hidden voice that you often ignore
- Reflect upon the wisdom of "the opposite side"
- Ponder the restlessness of the human heart

You have the opportunity to reflect upon twelve significant concepts that will call you to personal growth. As in Dr. Glenn's previous work, *Transform: Twelve Tools for Life,* the goal here is to make each concept immediately applicable. In this volume, we seek to fulfill the additional goal of influencing leadership effectiveness with concepts that reflect spiritual insights. Each chapter includes a journal entry; you must become engaged with the exercise to gain the value intended. In addition, each chapter provides a leadership challenge, a spiritual application, and a daily practice, which are all necessary components of successfully developing these concepts. Our hope is that you will fully engage yourself, personally apply these concepts, and begin to effectively lead from within.

Acknowledgments

I want to acknowledge the continuing and prayerful support of Elizabeth, my wife, and my daughter, Rebecca, for without their constant light in my life—a true reflection of God's grace for me—nothing would be possible. I would also like to thank Dr. James Guthrie, my professor and mentor in leadership, whose continued questioning and insights drive me to think deeper.

Tom Beeman

I am filled with gratitude to God for my son Christopher and the joy he gives to me. I would also like to acknowledge all those, including my coauthor, who have etched into my consciousness the intense desire to lead based on a higher calling.

Rich Glenn

Insight

*Do you know what amazes me
more than anything else—
the impotence of force to organize anything.
There are only two powers in the world—
the spirit and the sword;
and in the long run the sword
will always be conquered by the spirit.*

Napoleon Bonaparte

Chapter One

Know
Thyself

Leadership Challenge

Matthew stood up at a board meeting and read accusations written by a local newspaper columnist about the company's CEO, accusations that passed for news in the judgment of that weekly paper. Matthew, who owned a local business, said that he expected he would also come under attack if he were to make any public objection to the distortions reported in the article. Matthew did not intend any controversial purpose but sought to challenge several assertions that were appending evidence for the newspaper's allegations. It was not the first vicious article of a slanderous and gratuitous nature. He felt the board had a moral obligation to address some of the lies that were demoralizing the organization's workforce.

He announced that this meant more to him than his status in the eyes of the local media. Everyone was familiar with the words that Matthew read aloud, but the formal nature of his presentation made some board members uncomfortable. What was an organization to do when their CEO was subjected to this kind of intimidation so common in modern society?

Their CEO, the person who represented the very soul of the organization, was being called into question in a public forum. It's not an uncommon situation. Leaders serve as the moral compass for organizations and also their very public face. How leaders conduct themselves—the moral stands they take—leads and affects the entire organization.

So what was the appropriate action? The board members gave the CEO a strong vote of support, but the question remained: Should there be a public response? The CEO was left weighing his own response to the situation. He was certain that the allegations were false, but was concerned about how the public would interpret a denial or counter-argument.

Often those who seek to preserve their integrity for righteousness' sake will face the jeers of others. Hear these prophetic words from the Wisdom of Solomon:

> Let us lie in wait for the righteous man, because he is inconvenient to us and opposes our actions . . . He became to us a reproof of our thoughts; the very sight of him is a burden to us, because his manner of life is unlike that of others, and his ways are strange. We are considered by him as something base, and he avoids our ways as unclean; he calls the last end of the righteous happy, and boasts that God is his father. Let us see if his words are true, let us test him with insult and torture.
>
> (Wisdom of Solomon 2:12, 14–17, 19
> RSV Catholic Edition)

Know Thyself

A great deal of research about self-understanding is emerging today in psychological literature. Temperament and personality testing is routine in many organizational structures. Character traits and attributes are defined and measured for most leadership roles.

Is this leader a team player? Is there an understanding of how to develop and lead high-performing teams? Can this candidate build cooperation and collaborate with diverse groups? Can this person see the big picture? Is this a leader able to discern emerging trends and patterns, and can this person understand the systems entrusted to him or her? Integrity, leadership creativity, and relationship building are all becoming required competencies. Each will be addressed as we move forward.

Much emphasis is also placed on self-awareness issues. How does the leader become self-aware? How can we understand the meaning of our own strengths and weaknesses? What's the meaning behind self-esteem? Can a leader change those attributes in self that need to be changed to become more effective? Is there a blueprint, or are we all different? What role does ongoing learning play in one's development as a person and as a leader?

Leaders who discern that during life we are engaged in the task of making our souls ready for eternity are a different kind of leader.

We believe, however, that a larger context of meaning for life and work must be operative for the person who will lead others. Our model points to a deep, personal spiritual life that answers the question of why we are here and nurtures the spiritual resources for self and others. A leader must be able to reflect upon the mystery of being human and to create an environment that nurtures the spiritual development of others. St. Hilary reflected upon this mystery: "Before I came to know Thee, I was nothing. I did not know the meaning of life, and I had no understanding of myself."[1] His understanding came when God's love penetrated his heart.

We are created in God's image and likeness. We have a body and a soul—and that soul is a spirit endowed with intelligence and free will. The human soul is "the ultimate internal principle which animates our bodies and by which we feel, think and will."[2] Consider: I think and can reflect on that thinking. I can apprehend myself to be identical with the being who thinks. There is complete and perfect reflection of an agent back upon itself. This process is quite impossible for inanimate objects, e.g., a piano cannot play itself, an eye cannot see itself, and a scythe cannot cut itself.[3]

Scripture is replete with proof that the soul of a person is spiritual and immortal. A classic verse says, "And fear ye not them that kill the body, and are not able to kill the soul"

(St. Matt. 10:28). "How right, then, was Voltaire in saying: 'Materialism is the most enormous of all absurdities and the greatest folly that has entered the human mind.'"[4]

Leaders who discern that during life we are engaged in the task of making our souls ready for eternity are a different kind of leader. They are likely to understand the principle of sowing and reaping. These leaders are apt to deliberate before acting. In acting, they are accountable for their choices. They are also willing to take personal responsibility for their thoughts, words, and deeds. As Shakespeare expressed in *Othello* through the character of Iago:

> 'Tis in ourselves that we are thus or thus. Our bodies are our gardens, to the which our wills are gardeners; so that if we plant nettles, or sow lettuce, set up hyssop and weed up thyme, supply it with one gender of herbs, or distract it with many, either to have it sterile with idleness, or manured with industry, why, the power and corrigible authority of this lies in our wills (*Othello*, Act I, Scene iii).[5]

The knowledge of why we were made and what life really means creates a very different worldview for a leader. Perspective is based in a particular context: "And we know that to them that love God, all things work together unto good, to such as, according to his purpose, are called to be saints" (Rom. 8:28). This mind-set allows the leader to persevere and not complain about circumstances. We see that leaders who understand that they were created to serve and love God also accept a certain responsibility for their neighbor.

Without a proper understanding of self and sense of meaning and purpose, one cannot lead others.

Colleagues and coworkers of such leaders recognize that dignity in the workplace becomes an expectation—along with the work that promotes the glory of God. Indeed, God has a claim upon our lives—we belong to him. "Thou hast made us for Thyself, O Lord and our hearts are restless until they rest in Thee."[6]

Such an understanding acknowledges God's right to lay down the conditions as to how we must use the life he has given us.[7] A leader is one who guides and has influence. Without a proper understanding of self and a sense of meaning and purpose, one cannot lead others. This context of meaning for life allows leaders to ask themselves the following questions about work:

- Is our enterprise good (rather than does it pay)?
- Do we, who want to change the workplace, invite employees to grow through these changes?
- Does our work promote the glory of God, and does our workplace culture reflect the dignity of each employee?[8]

This framework also encourages leaders to answer this question: How can we help each other accomplish our duty, to serve the work? "If our hearts are not wholly in the work, the work will not be good—and work that is not good serves neither God nor the community."[9] Thus, leaders who have this same basis for life will take a deliberate, active approach in articulating a commitment to good work.

Knowing yourself is more than knowing that we as individuals differ from each other in fundamental ways. It is also more than the ability to grasp temperament and personality theories, however helpful they may be. It is based primarily on the question of our existence: Where did I come from? Why am I here? Where am I going? The contemplative answer to these questions forms the essential foundation for every great leader.

Fireside Chat

Rich: When we wrote this chapter about knowing yourself, we probably hit on something basic to life. But to leaders, it seems to be of special

importance. For the people who read this book, what does self-knowledge have to do with how a person leads?

Tom: Along with leading comes an issue about living. I believe, as it has been said, that a life that is not reflected on is a life that is not worth living. If you are not in touch with who you are, can you actually lead an organization? I consider knowing oneself as a process that evolves over a lifetime, and the discovery of self is really the realization of who we are in relationship to God. We could have called this chapter *Deum Gloriam*. When I was in school and being taught by the Jesuits, I would write that on my paper. I don't think I had any idea what I was really trying to say. However, I realized that unless I live my life giving everything to God's greater glory, my life will not be blessed nor will it be lived in the way that God has purposed.

As a leader, you must come to understand what your calling really is. It isn't the trappings of being a leader, it isn't the office, it isn't the cars, it isn't the prestige of the title, but it is recognizing the unique calling and responsibility of the organization that you're leading within society. You come to understand that it is not just about the organization you lead, but that the organization is in fact organic and made up of people. Those people are working out their own salvation through the work that they do. As a leader, you need enough comprehension of yourself to reflect on and assist other people in coming to know who they are. As they come to know themselves, they can come to know God and his purpose for their lives. I believe that all organizations are part of God's plan to bring us to him.

Rich: That's an interesting point. I remember the publisher of this book asked us when he first read the manuscript: "Why would you write a chapter like this?" We have talked about this several times, and perhaps one reason is to express and to expose our own vulnerability. We recognize that we are dependent creatures; we have our own weaknesses, and we, too, are working out our salvation. We have also come to understand that it is possible for people to close their eyes to the most pressing issues connected with themselves but with grave consequences. If there is a consideration to pass on to a person reading this chapter, it is this: there's a lot of inner work that needs to be done in order for us to be credible as leaders. Undoubtedly, we often see ourselves quite different from what we are.

> **We have to be willing to make choices in the leadership role and stand by them.**

Tom: I've joked about this before, but the person who needs the most work is the leader. When God gives out gifts and talents, he says to a very privileged and, therefore, very accountable group, "I'm going to make you leaders." It is, however, a difficult and lonely calling—it's just so personally challenging.

Rich: I think leaders will identify with that.

Tom: I have always said to God, "Why didn't you give me the gift of healing or something really neat?" because people seem to venerate that. Leadership so many times is not venerated but excoriated. I think that you and I have come to realize that.

Rich: We have. We have also talked about how wisdom is never really appreciated in its conception—only its results. When a leader makes decisions, it may be years before the wisdom of that decision is known. This is difficult in a society that expects immediate gratification. We see that in the presidential election, and of course it happens every four years. The visibility of a leader makes that person an easy target. So, we have to be willing to make choices in the leadership role and stand by them.

Tom: What do you think about presidential elections when people throw mud at each other? Do you believe that elections could be conducted without the mudslinging, and how would you approach that? Does leadership mean diminishing your opponent?

Rich: This is a great segue to the next chapter which deals with the issue of integrity. Why don't we hold that question for a bit, as we invite our readers to do the exercises in this chapter?

JOURNAL EXERCISE

Know Thyself

Write out a statement that articulates your personal philosophy about the meaning of life. Be brief. These are your early thoughts. Consider this meaning in relationship to your role as a leader. Ask yourself the following question:

- Does my life convey this philosophy, and is it worthy of my Creator?

On a weekly basis, add to these early thoughts. Do not be afraid to change it from time to time when your own thinking becomes clearer. Be sure this always has a personal application to leadership and your role or function in the workplace.

SPIRITUAL APPLICATION

Insight

Insight will often remind us how ignorant we are, how little we really understand ourselves at times, and how frequently we are closed to the truth. There are moments, however, when we see the vast unknown and realize the potential within others and ourselves. Leaders must seek to cultivate and explore this vast world that lies beyond the reach of the commonplace life of the routine.[10]

Insight can touch the depths and heights of the leader's soul. It comes at times unexpectedly—like a penetration of light upon the mind. Insight is an important virtue for the leader who will contemplate a deeper understanding of self. Grasping the inward nature of things, along with the capacity to discern, is a sign of character, not just intuition. It is the attribute of those willing to ponder, think, and learn. Insight is a penetration. It finds a trained mind fertile ground.

Self-knowledge is the prerequisite to any real growth in this matter. We cannot become great leaders without an understanding of who we are. "The entrance to the famous temple of Apollo at Delphi in old Greece, bore an inscription which read as follows: 'Know thyself!' Whoever inscribed those words must have had quite a deep insight into human nature."[11] Self-knowledge and insight are acquired through withdrawal, reflection, and solitude. Like all virtues, these require the leader to live an intentional and disciplined life.

> **Self-knowledge is the prerequisite to any real growth in this matter.**

DAILY PRACTICE

 At the end of each day take an account of your responsibility to yourself and seek to relate yourself to the service of God.

- Seek the joy that results from a life of goodness and a clear conscience. Remember that there is always consolation in the service of God.
- Seek the peace that is at rest with God, with others, and with yourself.
- Seek the ability to bear with others patiently and without resentment and irritation.
- Seek a posture of gratitude and thanksgiving for the gift of another day.

Chapter Two

Personal Integrity

Leadership Challenge

Susan was meeting with two of her directors behind closed doors. Both directors supervised a pool of venders who supplied companies with a large line of equipment needs. The three of them were discussing a problem that involved one of their venders. As they discussed the matter, they all realized that there were larger issues involved than the incident that brought them together.

Four weeks had passed since the vender in question quoted a price to his customer for leased equipment. The price quoted sealed the deal and allowed the customer to use the equipment immediately. When the first monthly fee was due on the leased equipment, the lease price was significantly greater than the quoted price. The vender explained to his customer that the quote given was only an estimate. In addition, one of the directors discussing the case set the actual lease price of the equipment based on updated and increase rate scales. The customer was upset and asked the vender to make good on his original promise. This customer had turned down an opportunity to work with another vender offering a price much more favorable than the current updated lease price.

As Susan met with her two directors, there was disagreement about how the case should be handled. Susan asked: "What is the right thing to do? What would serve justice and the highest good of all involved?" Their integrity and the dignity of the customer were at stake. No one was blamed for the incident, but they had to make a decision about what to do. What should their decision be?

Personal Integrity

Because our unity of personality demands the integration of its parts, there is always the possibility that we can break up ("dis-integrate") into discordant pieces. But what are these parts that must be integrated if the person is to be whole? There are many lines along which personality can be unified. There is the integrity between word and deed, friendship and fidelity, private life and public life, mind and body, head and heart. But the integrity that is perhaps most basic to a human being is the one that binds one's being to one's behavior, endowment to achievement, or giftedness to response.
—Donald DeMarco[1]

Completeness—the place where words and deeds overlap—that is integrity. At the dawn of this new era, this ancient concept is under assault. Once it was thought that a man must stand by his word. Words were to be uttered only when they were uttered in truth. Language had as its purpose, not deceit, but clarity and truth. Today, language has been sullied, manipulated, and sanitized. Even American presidents split hairs, refusing to be accountable for their actions. Scripture is clear on this point—be either hot or cold, but not lukewarm (Rev. 3:15). Benjamin Whichcote said, "Right and truth are greater than any power, and all power is limited by right."[2] Consider the words of Daniel O'Connor: "Nothing is politically right, which is morally wrong."[3] What, then, has created this politically correct climate where nothing is wrong except if you violate political correctness itself?

Personal integrity calls for an unbiased view of the self, unfettered by the filters of self-aggrandizement, avoidance of pain, or lack of accountability. It seeks to see self as God sees us. Thus we can proclaim with Timothy that we can face our God unashamed (2 Tim. 2:15). We have run the race, at times even suffering the consequences of our actions, but always, always took responsibility. There, deeply embedded in the soul is true personal integrity, the place where our actions and our words coalesce, enshrouded in our values. It is here, then, in this world's environment of self-worship, that we talk about personal integrity, which is the antithesis of self-worship.

When Christ criticized the religious leaders of his day, it was not for their lack of adherence to the law: it was for their cynicism and failure to follow its spirit. Laws were not set up to punish (though they can), but to protect. Christ knew what was written on their hearts. We see great compassion for the woman caught in adultery who seeks forgiveness—Christ tells her to go and sin no more. Yet he has little compassion for pride. Pride strikes at integrity because it puts self in the place of God as the center and objective of our lives. It is the refusal to recognize our status as creatures, and this refusal contaminates our relationship with the rest of creation. We then come to think of ourselves as superior with a preference for our own ideas, schemes, and techniques.

> **Integrity is a recognition that leadership is a divine vocation.**

Many actions fight against integrity—the duplicitous person who is given to deliberate deceptiveness in behavior or speech; the phony who gives a false impression of truth or authenticity; the person who has mixed motives for a deed or action; and the hypocrite who professes what is not held or believed but falsifies the message.

Integrity, however, for the faith-filled person, is a recognition that the role of leadership is a divine vocation—and we offer our work to God. That work displays a steadfast adherence to truth and one's ethical code. Persons of integrity are persons who are sound. They are upright and worthy of confidence. They also show common sense and good judgment. This prepares leaders to recognize God's wisdom, providence, and love as well. It frees leaders from worry, anxiety, scrupulosity, and perfectionism. We are not destined to become absorbed in our own affairs. We can turn from self-justification, self-righteousness, and deceit, never allowing another to suffer the blame for our faults. Integrity, unlike pride, will give no pretense to virtues we do not possess. Seeking, desiring, or relishing flattery or compliments will not be important to our office. Leaders who share in this commitment will learn to give credit to God for their talents, abilities, and accomplishments.

Leaders must also be intentional about their position in relationship to issues they must encounter and solve. This intention must be born of wisdom. Wisdom always provides information to a person of integrity. As persons of integrity, we have taken positions, thought thoughts, and hoped hopes based on our values. Values then, help us focus our vision of leadership. It is here in our values that we determine our commitments. These undertakings and their fulfillment constitute our personal integrity. It is our values, shaped by our belief systems and informed by virtue, that ultimately form what we call integrity. A lack of integrity, then, occurs when we fail to live up to commitments. Keeping them can be as simple as being where you said you would be. Or, as is often the case, breaking commitments is saying one thing and doing another. You obey the law but not its spirit. As a recent American president said, "Define sex."

Here, deeply embedded, is the character of a person. Structured on values, built by beliefs, informed by wisdom, character develops. Strength of character is demonstrated by the consistency between the beliefs and the actions. "It is the set of the soul that determines the goals, and not the calm or

> **Strength of character is demonstrated by the consistency between the beliefs and the actions.**

the strife."[4] For the person of integrity whose character has been formed by constancy and faith, it is not external events, but the set of the soul, as the poem eloquently terms it, that produces a person of trust. The world can be in chaos about them, but they stay steadfast in their pursuits. That does not mean, of course, that a person of integrity is inflexible, but one element is never compromised: that which forms the foundation of the soul—virtue. This assures that the motives, the powers, the actions, and the being of a person are gathered into a characteristic whole by a definitive moral and ethical commitment to truth.[5]

To fulfill this commitment, the leader learns to trust in the universal sovereignty of God. It requires heroic faith and openness to the transforming power of the grace and love of God. "This is a valid conclusion: He who holds to the truth holds to God. He who lies rebels against God and betrays the rational basis of experience."[6]

Fireside Chat

Tom: We're moving away from self-reflection toward reflection on personal integrity. A quote by Donald  DeMarco, which I really like, says that "the integrity that is perhaps most basic to a human being is the one that binds one's being to one's behavior."[7]

Rich: We've discussed this before, Tom. We've taught it in our classes at Vanderbilt University. It's the congruency between what we say and what we do. It is so basic to integrity, yet I'll risk throwing in a monkey wrench: Scripture says, "For a just man shall fall seven times and shall rise again" (Prov. 24:16). See the dilemma? We have this goal to strive for, on the one hand, of living lives of integrity, but on the other hand we are flawed. This is the challenge of leadership. I think the question you asked at the end of our last discussion on the presidential race points to the most challenging issue—defending your record. How many times does the electorate or the media really look at the data? How do we judge a decision that may not bear fruit for five or ten years? How many times do we really measure performance based on the whole of a person's record? Can people ever really do all they say they would do? As you know, this gives the person challenging for the office a huge advantage because that person is comparatively under the radar screen.

I'm reflecting on our experience as leaders together in an organization, and I'm realizing how much under the microscope we have been, especially you, because you are the person who heads the organization and who has been most visible. So, let me throw the question back to you—because I think this really speaks at the heart of the issue from personal experience. What is it like to have to make decisions and live with your behavior every day of your life knowing that it is part of public record?

Tom: It's really interesting because there is a sense that the person who is leading a faith-based organization somehow has to be sinless, while in fact, you are not a saint—not a finished product. You struggle with the same issues that everyone struggles with in the organization, yet you are held to a higher level of accountability than anyone else.

I have often prayed the Ignatian prayer, "Lord take my will, Lord take my reputation." However, on the other hand, you feel like Augustine in saying, "but not yet." When you are going through the experiences of being personally attacked, people are not reflecting on your record alone but on your humanity and sinfulness. It's sort of out there for everyone to see. People often want to believe everything bad about other people— particularly those in leadership. In addition to that, leaders in faith-based organizations—because the organizations, not necessarily the people, stand so much in contrast to society—make for easy targets.

Rich: What do you say to leaders out there who are proud of their performance, are proud of the way they've led, know something about who they are, are willing to live with what they've done, and are aware of their limitations, and suddenly there is an onslaught; there is an attack and they are taken to the cleaners by their organization, local leaders, or the media? What do you say to the person who is in the direct fire? Especially since we know that God is wont to teach those who are in earnest.

Tom: Well, the solace that I would give won't be immediate, because you feel such attacks very personally, but it goes back to knowing yourself, having a deep interior life of prayer, and realizing that our life in the spirit is eternal and we are not supposed to just live our lives for the finite time that we have on earth. On this earth, the very organizations that honor us today will dishonor us tomorrow. The honor that we seek is never honor on this earth, but it is the honor of trying to serve God. This is what really puts it into perspective for me. I am not living my life for now; I'm living my life for eternity and the perpetual presence of God. That is the only thing that gets me through. Personally, however, it is hurtful. The very people that you count on to support you sometimes disappoint you the most. Those situations require prayer. If you're looking for a return today, this is probably not the type of leadership model that you want to adopt.

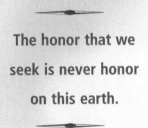

> The honor that we seek is never honor on this earth.

Rich: I guess basic to our philosophy would be our knowledge that if we fall short of what we say and what we do as leaders, there is hope through an amended life. We know that we can seek forgiveness and strive to change. We also know that there is a special blessing attributed to those people who are living a worthy life and are still under attack. We want to encourage leaders to claim the gospel of life that breathes with the vigor of a fresh energetic life from beginning to end. I hear you saying that the Bread of Life must feed us—must be our portion.

Tom: Yes. Therefore, a leader who is under attack certainly takes personal responsibility and accountability and makes acknowledgment. It sort of allays anyone's personal attack because you have already acknowledged it and then tried to move on. But do realize, as you indicated, that there are sometimes special blessings that go along with this because you are open to accept what comes from God.

Rich: Yes. As Plutarch said, "Socrates thought that if all our misfortunes were laid in one common heap, whence everyone must take an equal portion—most persons would be contented to take their own and depart."

We're going to be talking about leadership visibility in the next chapter and one truth we have certainly been able to recognize in our own lives is this: You really cannot hide when you're a leader. Once again, we are led to look beneath the surface of that which is going on around us and to see all as the machinery designed by God for the molding of character.

Journal Exercise

Personal Integrity

- How does integrity uphold good leadership in your own experience?
- Is there congruency between what you say and what you do?
- What is your decision when the right thing to do conflicts with what is profitable?
- Can success be gained the honest way? If so, what are the keys?

Spiritual Application

Prayer

To maintain this constancy of purpose in the pursuit of character development, God gave us a profoundly important gift: prayer. Prayer is a tool—a distinctly personal way to connect with God and also meditate on our beliefs, our relationship with those beliefs, and how we are, in fact, living them out. Spiritual leadership recognizes the sovereignty and absolute dominion of God and dependence on God—it is in prayer that this recognition is shown in practice.[8] It really is a check of our integrity; it is a way to correct course and get in touch with where we are. Prayer is an interactive activity with both God and us as giver and receiver. In the intimacy of prayer we can realize the true nature of our soul and its integrity.

Those who ridicule prayer ridicule one of the deepest instincts in human nature. Early in 1918, when the German offensive was threatening to bring defeat to the Allies in World War I, General Foch was appointed generalissimo on the western front. The time chosen for the great counter-offensive, which was to result in the victorious conclusion of the war, was dawn of July 18. The previous evening, Foch left Allied general headquarters, asking to be allowed an undisturbed hour to himself. He had been absent some time when a dispatch rider came with a message of such importance that the staff officers felt that General Foch should be informed. They looked for him in his billet, but he was not there. However, his orderly, knowing the general's habits, led them to the village church. There they found Foch kneeling motionless before the altar.[9]

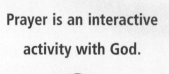

Prayer is an interactive activity with God.

Some argue that prayer is not necessary because God already knows our needs. Prudent leaders will, however, follow the example of Christ who showed that he wished for us to lay our requests before him: "And he spoke also a parable to them, that we ought always to pray, and not to faint . . . will not God revenge his elect who cry to him day and night . . . ?" (Luke 18:1, 7).

If you would endure with patience all the adversities and challenges of your honored role, be a person of prayer; be a leader with integrity.

DAILY PRACTICE

 At the end of each day, recall the promises you made for the day and all that you said you would do. Even a phone call unreturned when promised is a breach against integrity. Get in the habit of filling out a three-by-five-inch index card each night after a thoughtful examination of your day. Be intentional about beginning the next day by addressing the items from your card that were not dealt with the day before.

Learn to integrate this exercise with your evening prayer, and seek God's help in doing the difficult tasks that must be done.

Chapter Three

Don't Hide and Do Seek

Leadership Challenge

John was a rationalist. He was the kind of leader who was able to add ingenuity and logic to ideas and actions. He was a visionary and a builder. It was important to John that others saw him as competent and logical. He wanted to be acknowledged for his strategic analysis and capacity in relationship to complex issues. He was even known outside the organization for his expertise.

Unfortunately, John was rarely available to his organization or his staff. John was so involved in community, regional, and national initiatives, he failed to invest the necessary time into his own company. Threads were beginning to unravel. Leadership for organizational projects was lacking. The executive team felt abandoned and morale was at an all-time low. Blame was on the rise, risk-taking was on the decline, and work quality was taking a nosedive.

John's absence left a number of voids. Relationships suffered because no one had a pipeline to John. Great instability existed in the areas of trust and communication. The leadership team was not sure of itself and had no real direction from their leader. There was little knowledge of the goals and what to do. The team did not feel the freedom to do as it saw fit. Personal meaning also declined, as there was little feedback about individual contributions.

John's leadership style was an "I'll-hide-and-you'll-have-to-try-and-find-me" approach. It wasn't working.

Don't Hide and Do Seek

Visibility and availability are at the heart of effective leadership. Leaders create value through communication, which includes the visibility of their presence. Jeffrey J. Fox calls this "promoting yourself within the organization."[1] This ought not to be invasive or imposing; rather, it is based in humility. We are speaking about a posture of charity toward our neighbor, meaning the leader's intention of seeking the highest good for others. We would call this a very welcoming presence.

This presence inspires confidence, which grows out of the leader's ability to be seen, heard, and believed. "A leader has two important characteristics; first, he is going somewhere; second, he is able to persuade other people to go with him."[2] The person who leads needs to be credible and creative. Inspiring confidence necessitates determining results. Leaders must be clear that if they cry "forward," they must not fail to make plain in what direction to go.[3] Those in leadership positions must consciously and consistently choose the results they want to see manifested.[4]

A leader develops trust across a network of constituencies and understands what motivates others. This understanding has relational aspects. A leader can't hide in an organization but must seek to be with people—to listen deeply, to respect others, to build relationships, and to do what is just and best for the whole.

A leader's visibility also provides opportunity to model appropriate behavior and to manifest the values which drive the organization. The leader conveys the mission and makes it visible through personal witness, which can influence and shape the culture, promote collaboration, inspire quality outcomes, and assure that the workplace remains faithful to values. Leaders carry a great burden. They are often held to a higher standard than others.

Visibility must also know its limitations. It can be effective when, in balance with absence, it gives the organization the appropriate space and distance it needs to carry on the work. The leaders must learn to flow from visibility and availability to private reflection. Insight is gained through this active-reflective model. This contributes to the leader's ability to be teachable, self-critical, and accountable. Yet it allows the leader not to take self too seriously. Distance and reflection will offer the leader needed perspective, including the ability to enjoy the work and be open to the unexpected.

As Margaret Wheatley puts it, "Were we to become truly good scientists of our craft, we would seek out surprises, relishing the unpredictable when it finally decided to reveal itself. Surprise is the only route to discovery, the only path we can take if we're to search out the important principles that can govern our work."[5] Wheatley is referring to leadership and its impact on organizational culture when she asks, "Wouldn't we all welcome more laughter in the halls of management? I would be excited to encounter people delighted by surprises, instead of the ones I now meet, who are scared to death of them."[6] Leaders would do well to be seekers of truth, regardless of what they may encounter. Such discovery leads to a greater understanding of our roles and the mystery of our potential as well as the potential of others.

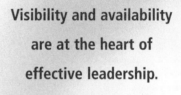

Visibility and availability are at the heart of effective leadership.

Discovery and visibility enable us to go beyond merely being available as a leader and actually to be present to real needs. Such a presence seeks to honor, understand, affirm, and recognize others' worth. It allows the leader to learn from others. It teaches the leader the value of collaboration. It helps the leader trust and respect others. It improves morale. It encourages everyone's contribution. It results in personal value through relationships and service.

Since leaders are encouraged to think from a system's perspective (seeing each part in relationship to the whole), to see the big picture, and to inspire a lofty vision, they must learn to focus attention on the important issues that affect the system and seek to understand them. This involves respecting and making visible the collective wisdom of the organization and maintaining an openness to other points of view. By highlighting the wisdom of the organization from a system's perspective, the leader visibly commits to supporting a learning organization. Jim Collins calls this Level 5 Leadership, where "leaders channel their ego needs away from themselves and into the larger goal of building a great company."[7]

> **Out of sight, out of mind is a dangerous axiom.**

Out of sight, out of mind is a dangerous axiom for any leader who seeks influence and success. Being present to our colleagues is a strong indication that we value them and respect their contribution. The leader signals a clear commitment to participative management when visible. More important, people feel they are very much a part of the organization. As Wheatley has observed, "The more (people) feel part of the organization, the more work gets done."[8] It is also not just about work but about life—so much of our lives is spent within organizations; it is here we must discover what is real and authentic about ourselves.

Since leaders are often encouraged to be risk takers, we encourage leaders to begin taking risks at the level of relationships, since "leadership skills have also taken on a relational slant."[9] The risk is that we will not only be more visible to others but more willing to invest in them. Every human heart longs to be appreciated and gains self-respect through growth. Develop human capital and see how quickly problems can be solved. As George MacDonald has said, "Man's rank is his power to uplift."[10]

One last thought about leadership, visibility, and the development of relationship. "Interpersonal ineptitude in leaders lowers everyone's performance: It wastes time, creates acrimony, corrodes motivation and commitment, builds hostility and apathy."[11] As a leader, don't hide from people, but do seek to pay attention to the developmental needs of your associates, enhancing their abilities, and elevating their status as people who are called to work that has dignity.

Perhaps the greatest example of don't hide and do seek is the mystery of the incarnation. God comes to us reconciling us to himself, bending down from heaven and touching us in the flesh. In this one act alone, we see manifest these traits of leadership: great humility, personal responsibility, and love for those entrusted to our care.

Fireside Chat

Tom: You know, Rich, in this chapter, we make the statement that every human heart longs to be appreciated and gains self-respect through growth. In our situation, you have been the one in the organization who really helps us invest in people and recognize that this ministry is about everyone's gifts. I thought maybe you could reflect on your work in helping to make that human investment which is so critical to an organization's success.

Rich: It may be what sets organizations apart. We have often talked about the development of our people as the greatest competitive advantage that we have. We would challenge and encourage leaders to give thought to that. I also remember our conversations about our pride in the work we do. You mentioned earlier about doing our work to the glory of God, and we know that the work we do in health care has great dignity. In one of his earlier encyclicals, Pope John Paul II mentioned not only the dignity of the work but the dignity of the worker as well. You and I have come to the point where we are just as proud of emphasizing the dignity of the worker as we are in our reaching out to heal the sick. Although the work has great dignity and is the call of the gospel to us, the person that does that work has great dignity as well, and what better way to ratify our commitment than to invest in our employees?

I am struck by the George McDonald quote that "Man's rank is his power to uplift." I know you have always made it a priority in your leadership style to convey the message that you want to uplift your colleagues, and in a sense it is an invitation for everyone to assume a part in a leadership role. So, part of what makes us visible in the organization is not only that we are present to people in a physical way but also that we are present to them in supporting their careers. It is really their vocation; every person has a vocation to fulfill. There is some work that God has for each person, and in doing that, not only is God glorified but also that person is recognized as one who is unique and especially qualified by God to do that job.

Tom: Rich, there was a movie made several years ago that is probably the best war movie I've seen. It's called *We Were Soldiers*. No matter what you think about the war in Vietnam, I think that Lieutenant Colonel Hal Moore, the character played by Mel Gibson, has some interesting insights into leadership that are relevant here as far as the discussion about rank and the responsibility of a leader.

He talked about leading from the front. If you have had the opportunity to see the movie, you know he was the first person off the helicopters and the last person back on. During the movie, he made an interesting reflection. Someone said to him, "Weren't you worried about being killed?" (It was a horrific battle, where they fought an army ten times their number. They not only prevailed but every person on the American side got off the battlefield—Moore brought his dead and wounded back.) And the Moore character said, "I wasn't afraid of being killed. I had a mission to perform and God was going to determine whether I lived or died."

His responsibility was his mission toward his people, and he and the noncommissioned officer, whose name I forget, demonstrated what true leadership is in the midst of battle. They directed their men, they stayed with them, they instructed them, they held them up, they made sure that they performed their duty, and they enabled them to leave the battlefield feeling good about what they had done. In a lot of respects that is leadership: to focus first on the mission and not on whether you are going to get hurt. I thought that was an excellent example. And interestingly enough, Hal Moore, who is now in his eighties, is a very faith-based leader.

Rich: That's a great example of leadership. Actually, a few years ago we saw that movie together with our wives. I remember Moira saying after the movie that he was the kind of person she would want leading her in such circumstances. Do you remember the journalist/photographer that was there with them in Vietnam? There was a specific encounter between that photographer and Lieutenant Colonel Moore. Rather than seeing this photographer as a second-class citizen, you might remember how he showed him great respect. They built a relationship of sorts. At the end of that movie, before Lieutenant Colonel Moore steps back on the helicopter, he said to that photographer that it would be hard for him to forgive himself since so many of his men died and he didn't. Here was a leader who was not only visible to his people but he had the capacity to completely identify with each person. You saw that every man was a part of his team, and his investment in them was paramount.

> You may not always be physically present, but they know that you are there.

Tom: I think this is a particularly important discussion in this chapter where we talk about don't hide and do seek. I think the character that Mel Gibson played was a person who did not hide; he was utterly present during the entire battle to every one of his soldiers. That is profound because I think that is what leadership is. You may not always be physically present, but they know that you are there. Your leadership is solid and you are urging them on, and that is the kind of person that people want to follow.

Journal Exercise

Don't Hide and Do Seek

Create a map of your organization by department, keeping in mind those people who influence others. Decide strategically your movement around the map to cover the entire territory on a daily basis. Mark out on the map your journey and date where you have been each day.

The map will give you a visual image of where to proceed. Each year create a new map design of the organization. Save your maps from year to year. They will tell a story of how visible you are and how consistent you have been.

Spiritual Application

Resolution

Being visible and present to others is not easy for many of us. In fact, certain personality types are reluctant to exhibit themselves socially. This stems not from a lack of regard for others but a basic orientation that is more focused on the inner world. These people are often called introverts. Introverts are capable of rich social activity and deep relationship building—but generally on a smaller scale. On the other hand, an extrovert may find it easier to be visible and present to others but may be less patient and suffer from a form of shallowness if interactions are constant.

Resolution will help any temperament type. When we resolve to do something, we choose to discipline ourselves in relationship to certain actions. This act of determination commits the leader to a decision. Being resolute is a virtue that indicates one's trustworthiness. Leaders, therefore, must discipline themselves around such resolutions. It is essential that the leader create practices that support decisions to be more available to the team or the organization. Our calendars reflect our commitment to others. Being generous with our time is not a waste of time. Every minute we invest in another will bring back a great return—either it will provoke greater loyalty toward us and from us or it will enhance our character.

> **Every minute we invest in another will bring back a great return.**

William Hazlitt has said that there is nothing more to be esteemed than a firmness and decision of character.[12] This is resolution. One more thought: "There is no exercise better for the heart than reaching down and lifting people up."[13]

Daily Practice

Look at the map from the previously outlined exercise. Begin each day by making five contacts from the day before. This need only take minutes. Write a quick note, send some e-mails, or make a few calls to follow up your prior day's activity with short messages of appreciation and encouragement to those with whom you came in contact. Over a thousand contacts will be made during the course of a year, and it will only cost you fifteen minutes each morning.

Awareness

If objective reality means God,
then we had better conform to him,
and it is silly to try to make him conform to us.

Peter Kreeft

Chapter Four

One's Viewing Point

Leadership Challenge

Steve was the top fund-raiser for his company. His vice president recognized Steve's accomplishments several times during the past year. In fact, Steve made the vice president's job in relationship to fund-raising a lot easier.

There was a catch, however. Steve was notorious for walking over people in the organization. He was rude and uncooperative with other departments. Many described him as arrogant. Those within the organization who had to collaborate with Steve found it unbearable. Several of Steve's coworkers left the organization complaining about his lack of respect and questioning the organization's values, since it appeared that the organization was willing to ignore such behavior as a trade-off for financial results.

Increasingly, the problem could not be ignored. The vice president was confronted about several situations that led to coworkers' departures. Each time, the vice president defended Steve and insisted the problem was not that severe. Suddenly the entire development department—Steve's fellow fund-raisers—walked out in protest, leaving Steve alone to raise sums that even he could not attain.

The vice president still protested, yet he was now facing his own crisis. He had held Steve in high esteem for what Steve was able to do for him. He had lost his objectivity in the process and had a viewing point that was too close to the situation. Like trying to watch a TV screen from too close a distance, this vice president's point of view was clouded by his viewing point. Others could clearly see what was happening. Here, an intelligent and respected leader had lost perspective and held a point of view that was increasingly challenged by the work culture.

Unless this vice president can step back and view this from a more advantageous viewing point, his point of view will soon undermine employees' trust and this slippage in the matter of integrity will hinder his ability to lead.

One's Viewing Point

Everyone has a point of view. It is a construct of one's intellectual, emotional, and spiritual development. Leaders are expected to have a point of view on almost every topic. It is assumed that these points of view are based on knowledge, but are they? We believe leaders must adhere to the science of the ultimate order of the universe (metaphysics). "It is the highest human wisdom and it has its foundation in the fact that God made all things according to the pattern of his wisdom. We see that pattern with our intellects as they are perfected by common sense."[1] Wisdom and common sense mean that leaders will be intentional about their position on the issues they must encounter and solve. This intention must be born in wisdom.

Scripture, therefore, is a consideration in our discussion since we are told that God's view is based on a singularly unique viewing point. God does not see the world with the limited view we have as human beings. Thus, there are spiritual implications related to a viewing point that will influence one's point of view. One may argue, for instance, that petty theft from a large company that can afford to lose a few dollars is not a big deal. Virtue, however, dictates that this point of view is tainted by an unethical frame of reference as a viewing point.

Our own points of view reveal much about ourselves. We call these mental models which determine how we see and view the world because they reveal our deeply held beliefs and assumptions. The Germans called this *Weltanschauung*, meaning a comprehensive philosophy based on one's view of the world and human life. Examining our viewing point in relationship to each mental model we hold is a powerful way of addressing flawed mental models.[2]

Temperament also challenges our mental models as leaders concerning our points of view and what we know. Each temperament has an attraction toward certain data. Some temperaments assess quickly the details of a situation but are blind to the bigger picture—while others are inclined to take in a more global view. This means some can see a particular event in relationship to other events that are taking place around it.

One's point of view may not mean much without an understanding of one's *viewing point*. In concert with revealed truth, objective reality, reason, and temperament, character is a crucial element of awareness and insight that can impact a leader's effectiveness.

Since leaders are entrusted with responsibility, they need to develop a model which encourages them to reexamine their viewing point. A perspective formed but not based on a good solid viewing point has no real contribution to desired results. One's viewing point thus becomes intrinsic to any successful leadership model.

> **We come to trust our point of view based on our viewing point.**

To illustrate: a runner circling the bases in a baseball game will slide into home plate. There will be a different point of view as to whether the runner is safe or out. The team we root for, our favorite players being involved in the action, our personal involvement in the play, or even where we are sitting can influence these perspectives. In each of these, we have a specific viewing point. The umpire has a particularly advantaged viewing point which influences his point of view because he witnesses the play from close proximity. A fan in the stands in the lower levels has a viewing point that is not as advantaged as the umpire's. The upper deck fan is even less advantaged. Ironically, some situations will demand that our viewing point be from a distance in order to gain an advantage. These are the times when being further from an issue gives us a healthier objectivity.

> The biggest disadvantage to a proper viewing point is subjectivism.

We come to trust our point of view, therefore, based on our viewing point. A corporate decision about finances might well be suspect if the decision is based on a non-finance professional's viewing point. To illustrate further: would we listen to one's point of view about settling a dispute if that person did not know the facts of the dispute itself?

Without a proper viewing point our point of view is limited. It may even be empty. Leaders must position themselves to have the best viewing point possible if their point of view is to be taken seriously. Such a position involves educational considerations, relationship skills, capacity to discern and reflect on the issues involved, and having reliable and relevant information. Everyone is entitled to a point of view, but only those with a proper viewing point will be taken seriously. This is not to dishonor any individual leader but to assure that leaders have a point of view informed by wisdom. A correct viewing point is an essential part of a leader's toolbox.

A poor viewing point may be the result of ignorance, a misinformed strategic plan, a lack of information, relational contamination, political issues, budgetary pressure, an unclear vision, or a simple lack of motivation. We propose, however, that the biggest disadvantage to a proper viewing point is subjectivism. It is the denial of the intellect and the placing of absolute trust in one's senses that drives decisions away from the realm of reason and objective truth.

The next time you are asked about your point of view, explain clearly your viewing point and address the issue based on the strength and advantage that the viewing point gives you. By explaining our viewing point, we are identifying the context for our point of view.

Another example will illustrate the point. A group of historians writing about the life of a famous philosopher had different points of view based on their own research, data, and opinions. When a journal, penned by the philosopher himself, was discovered, their points of view were challenged based on this personal disclosure—a somewhat unique viewing point to say the least. A further contribution by the philosopher's closest disciple was discovered that gave a second unique viewing point. These two findings shifted the historians' opinions because they were given new, somewhat unique viewing points.

When you evaluate your own effectiveness with a team or an organization, ask yourself, what is my viewing point in relationship to the team or to the organization? If you are in the upper deck far from the action you may want to reexamine your ability to influence through your own point of view. And again, if you are not playing by the rules, given the ethical guidelines that govern your work, you will quickly forfeit your right to influence and to lead.

Fireside Chat

Rich: We have spent a lot of time now on issues about the person of the leader. We've talked about character and  the soul of a person; we've examined the leader's sense of self; we've discussed the visibility of the leader, and now we're starting to discuss how the leader thinks—the kind of tools that are needed to lead. In this chapter we have considered a person's judgment and how a person uses some of the intellectual tools he or she has. As a leader who has led multiple organizations for twenty-five years now, how do you discern the truth? How do you discern what's best for an organization—the choices you have to make, the decisions that are constantly at your door? How do you use tools like the one we talked about here that really ask leaders to reflect on their viewing points?

Tom: Well, that's a very provocative question, and I would tell you that, had you asked me twenty-five years ago when I started in leadership, I would have been utterly unprepared to answer it. And, I'm not sure I'm ready now, but I can tell you about the discernment model that I try to employ for myself. I think that you start with the fundamental issues around the virtues. Those virtues are formulated in the mind. You refer to four cardinal virtues in your *Transform* book, which I think are fundamental to all of existence. Prudence, wisdom, temperance, and fortitude were not only embedded in Christianity but were also identified by the ancient philosophers as extraordinarily important. I think that as those virtues are identified, and as you move toward those virtues, you come to recognize where you may lack in a particular virtue. For example, in my life my challenge has always been fortitude. I've never had a major issue of temperance—well, maybe on a few occasions—but to really stick with something—how can I embrace fortitude and build on it so it becomes a stronger virtue in my life? That is one of the key elements for me. I really do believe that there are a group of factors that influence a person's decisions.

One of the very basic elements is family. Family helps determine personal values. Then there are, I think, some innate elemental values that are embedded into the human psyche. It seems that all cultures, for example, agree that homicide or murder is wrong. These are embedded in the conscience of all of us. Then we have the social setting and community in which a person grows up. Next we have education and profession. What are the values of a particular profession and organization that help us make decisions?

And finally, religious beliefs and faith are the foundation. All of those help comprise the discernment model in the way a faith-based person makes decisions. I like to reflect back and hope that my faith, my family—those elemental virtues—are instructing me no matter what happens. Political and organizational values are not so overarching that they come into conflict with the beliefs I hold personally.

Once I make a decision that takes me away from myself—away from my convictions—I am in trouble.

Rich: I'm thinking, Tom, of leaders who may not be in a faith-based organization, and the pressure is extreme for them to make a profit. There are stockholders and others who have a vested interest in certain results. The values, or the lack thereof, that are exemplified in that organization may not support that person's personal quest to be a man or woman of faith and integrity, and one who has a viewing point that is congruent with the Gospels. What do we say to a person who is trying to live a life where society and organizations don't support personal values?

Tom: That's a great question. First, don't let me mislead anybody that faith-based organizations have all the answers. There are as many potentially distracting politics and issues within faith-based organizations as there are in other organizations.

Rich: Which is sometimes, therefore, more difficult for the person of faith because there is the appearance of support by a system that is congruent with them. Thus, some false idea of support may mar a noble life.

Tom: I think that is right on. I think that in any organization, people who have developed skills, self-knowing, and prayerful lives can use those elements of self-knowledge and faith to help them evaluate and discern what is right. I really like that quote you always use: "Listen to the one clear, distinctive voice within yourself." Listen to that voice, and if what you are being asked to do, or are doing, is incongruent with what you believe is right, then it probably is not right. Then you may have to say "no" within your organization, which may gain you a tremendous amount of respect or criticism. You may not be a good fit for that organization. By staying, you could lose your soul. To me, losing my soul would be the worst possible thing. I would say that the discernment model in chapter 7—and I would urge everyone to look at that chapter—skillfully helps filter one's decision making.

Rich: Maybe a red flag for leaders who read this chapter is that the decisions they make today—if, in fact, leaders can lose their souls based on a decision—can influence an entire career. Once I make a decision that takes me away from myself—away from my convictions—I am in trouble. Sooner or later I will have some false idea of the character of God because I will make excuses that bend God's will to mine. Whenever our idea of God falls short, our own character is certain to fail also.

Tom: I agree with that, and I pray that Providence will always bring leaders back. But as you create shell after shell, as you make decisions that are not consistent with virtue, it is very hard to turn back over time.

Rich: There is a Dorian Gray[3] quality to every leader's life.

Tom: Sort of scary, isn't it?

Rich: It is. Unless a leader is willing to look in a mirror, the viewing point will never change, but the results will be clear for everyone to see.

Journal Exercise

One's Viewing Point

Consider a strong opinion you hold and your position in relationship to it. Consider the following questions:

- What informs you about your point of view?
  - What is the real data?
- How did you reach a conclusion about your point of view?
- Have you considered other points of view?
- What are the viewing points behind these opinions?
- Does anyone who could advise you have a more advantageous viewing point?

Spiritual Application

Common Sense

The Book of Wisdom says, "temperance, prudence, justice, and fortitude are the most profitable things in life" (WS 8:7). Many philosophers, such as Aristotle, Plato, Socrates, and Cicero, had a clear knowledge of the cardinal virtues. "Plato assigns to them the primacy in his *Ideal State*, and Cicero deduces all the other virtues from them."[4] Common sense is allied to prudence, which purposes all one's actions to bear in mind our true end.[5]

Common sense is the ability to make judgments according to the ordinary rules of conduct.[6] Seeing the truth clearly is essential to our discussion of one's point of view. Making good decisions, based on common sense and assisted by prudence, will strengthen our viewing point for all future contemplation.

For the wise men of old, the cardinal problem of human life was how to conform the soul to objective reality, and the solution was wisdom, self-discipline, and virtue. For the modern, the cardinal problem is how to conform reality to the wishes of man, and the solution is a technique.[7]

Contrast this idea with the Old Testament Book of Tobias, which says:

Seek counsel always of a wise man. Bless God at all times: and desire of him to direct thy path, and that all thy counsels may abide in him.

(Tob. 4:19–20)

Common sense says that the inferior should conform to the superior. God does not see situations as we see them. Seeing them from God's viewing point is the basis for virtuous leadership.

Daily Practice

Pick an object that can be seen from multiple locations. For example, look at a rose from a distance. Do you get the full picture? Does the smell and elegance of the rose make its greatest impact upon you from afar? Hold the rose in your hand and bring it up to your eyes. Again, notice that some of the particulars are lost. The petals are too close to see their shape and their beauty. Even the smell at this distance might be too strong for some.

> **Seeing from God's viewing point is the basis for virtuous leadership.**

Continue to experiment with the rose and your distance from it. Notice when the rose has its greatest impact upon your senses. Notice how you see the rose differently from varying viewing points. Also notice how changing viewing points contributes to your appreciation of the rose's beauty.

We all do this when taking a simple picture. We change our viewing point until it enables us to capture the picture in its most advantageous light. Many times, multiple cameras take the same pose but from slightly different angles, or viewing points. It is amazing to see how just a different angle can affect the results.

Take stock of where you stand in relationship to an issue; in other words, always consider your viewing point before locking in your point of view.

Chapter Five

The Integrated Brain

Leadership Challenge

Ed was reading his e-mails. A complaint was addressed to him personally as the CEO. The person writing to Ed accused human resources of unfair pay practices based on age discrimination. Ed had received numerous complaints about that department and decided to take this matter into his own hands.

Responding to the e-mail, Ed invited the complaining party to meet with him later in the week. Ed heard an impassioned appeal to straighten out the mess in human resources, specifically the inequity in pay practices that was directly affecting this worker. Ed was emotionally drawn to the injustice he perceived was involved in this person's story. He followed up with a meeting between himself and the vice president for human resources.

Making a number of assumptions based on his emotional response to the employee complaint, Ed drew some conclusions that created confusion and turmoil. Ed had not thought through the situation carefully and sabotaged policy, protocol, and respect for how the organizational structure defined roles. As the leader of the company, Ed had acted on emotion apart from reason and undermined his own leadership staff. The human resources department now realized that anyone in the company who had a complaint went directly to Ed—and had been for some time.

Further exploration revealed that human resources was facing obstacles based on Ed's leadership style. It became clear that Ed had frequently intervened and acted independently, making arbitrary decisions that would override policy. Human resources was left to pick up the mess. The salary structure had been sabotaged by the leader based on his inability to think with both sides of the brain.

Ed must work on the virtue of prudence and give greater forethought to his actions. Prudence enables us to choose good means to a good end.[1] How could Ed's concern for employees have been positive? What response should Ed have given to those who appealed to his office?

The Integrated Brain

According to modern researchers, the brain is divided into two hemispheres known as the left brain and the right brain. Another way of describing this dynamic is to say that there is one brain with two strategies. The left brain is the sequential processor of information. It is here that our brain makes rules, alerts us to dangers, and analyzes situations. This is the intellectual side of the brain where reason and the will make decisions to implement ideas. Leaders are expected to spend a significant amount of time here, in the realm of reason. It is important to think through issues and to break them down into critical components. Leaders must also be aware of the history and context of issues, with all the supporting data and facts related to them. These are left-brain functions.

The left side of the brain is known for being more objective, rational, and definitive as well. The left brain prefers to avoid surprises, finds it difficult to admit wrongdoing, punishes others' mistakes, and often dwells on the past. There is a time orientation to left-brain thinking. The left side of the brain dislikes any confusion and would like to make fairly quick decisions followed by closure.

Right-brain thinking is more subjective and tends to be more emotional and feeling oriented. The right-brain thinker contemplates an issue and asks: Who is going to be affected by our decision and how? The right-brain thinker considers the impact on individuals. Service and justice become important focuses. The right hemisphere also contains the artistic side of the person and is often the field of nonverbal functions (i.e., painting, drawing, and playing sports). The right side of the brain usually takes more risks, likes surprises, and can accept being wrong. It can also break the rules. The right side of the brain is open and creative. It can tolerate confusion but can be impetuous. Right-brain thinkers look into the future and usually don't look back. There seems to be a connection between right-brain thinking and emotional intelligence.

Emotional intelligence is often associated with soft skills in the workplace because of the abilities associated with it. According to Daniel Goleman, these learned capabilities are reflected in personal and social competencies.[2] Personal competence determines how we manage ourselves (self-awareness, self-regulation, and motivation). Social competence dictates how we handle relationships (empathy, social skills). Coincidently, the right side of the brain houses emotional awareness and the ability to tune into emotional currents. While left-brain thinking looks squarely at the issue at hand and asks how to solve it, right-brain thinking considers the factors surrounding the issue and asks how we will respond to these matters as well.

Virtuous leadership is not limited to either the left or right hemispheres of the brain.

One particular structure in the brain called the amygdala is identified more and more with the emotional brain because it is the site of all emotional memory. The amygdala can create problems because it can hijack our reactions based on what researchers call memory matches. If the amygdala finds a match, it reacts behaviorally the way it has always done when faced with similarly emotionally charged information. The amygdala causes snap judgment and emotional reactions before our intellect or reasoning has the chance to react.

In light of this information, even the left-brain thinker must contend with the emotional hijacking of the amygdala. This may be a blind area for the typical left-brain thinker. The right-brain thinker, who is already emotionally sensitive, must be on guard not to lose sight with reality; they need to guard against making emotional decisions apart from the facts. Good judgment respects both brain functions.

> **Integrating the heart into our thinking can bring virtue to the intellect.**

Virtuous leadership is not limited to either the left or right hemispheres of the brain but comes from an integration of both left- and right-side capacities to assure a healthy balance between the objective and subjective and between reason and feeling. A leader's decision and an action plan must, therefore, respect and address factual issues, including financial considerations, while paying attention to other possibilities, and new ways of thinking, that challenge old mental models along with a wider impact from a systems perspective.

When we encourage people to be integrated brain thinkers, we are referring to the proper use of all brain functions. Leaders must think about the implications of both hemispheres and of the two strategies that flow from the one brain. Effective leaders can tap either side of the brain based on need and circumstance. They need to feel comfortable in both worlds since they must live in both worlds. It simply will not fly for a leader to say, "Oh, but I am a left-brain thinker," to excuse a lack of empathy or relationship building. At the same time, a leader must never abrogate his or her responsibility to make decisions based on sound reasoning and good logic.

Integrated intelligence combines reason, the will, and the emotions to carry out the office of leadership. Some experts would also use language that introduces the heart. In other words, a leader must think with both head and heart.

Pascal said, "that the heart has reasons that reason knew not of." Integrating the heart into our thinking can bring virtue to the intellect. A prudent leader is both humble and docile—both influenced by the voice of the heart. Chip Dodd has called the voice of the heart a call to full living.[3] He says, "We do things because we ought to instead of awakening to the desires within our hearts that hunger for truth and hunger to do things because we passionately desire to do them."[4] The heart can also be identified as the seat of the will. It is the human heart that makes decisions and puts action into motion.[5]

Whether we attribute the dynamic to left and right brain hemispheres or to the heart-mind connection, it is clear that without this integration we will be impeded as leaders. Leaders must be competent, prudent, and responsible to be sure. They must be able to move processes forward and solve difficult problems. Leaders cannot forget, however, that patience and diligence are virtues. Considering long-term implications and learning from problems before trying to solve them has great value. Leaders must learn to think differently. The capacity for creativity, compassion, and vulnerability will build character and strengthen relationships. Integration is a call for the leader to become fully human. Knowing how to use the resources of the mind is a virtue, and integration of brain functions is key to the process.

Fireside Chat

Tom: Rich, this chapter deals with the integrated brain. You might say it is the first scientific chapter of the book.

It examines the left side and the right side of the brain. Our readers might be curious as to why this was included, and I wonder if you could give some insights as to not only why it was included but also how the right-brain and left-brain functions help us deal with issues about leadership and the thought processes of leaders.

Rich: We have discussed how leaders reflect the organization that they lead. Every organization probably has departments, functions, and roles that are both left and right brain. For some reason, there is always difficulty integrating the departments that reflect those two functions in the same way that it is difficult for some people to integrate the two functions in themselves.

One of the reasons that we included this chapter in the book is because leaders, if they look at the activity of their organization, are going to see both of these functions at work. To be successful, they need to ensure that excellence can be identified with both functions within the organization. If you make a lot of money but don't know how to solve your personnel problems, pretty soon the people who helped you make all that money aren't around anymore, or they are so disgruntled they find a way to sabotage the future.

When we look at any organization, one can see those employees referred to as the soft-skilled people and those that do the "real work." In some organizations, for example, it might be the conflict between marketing and manufacturing. We see, in effect, something that's most likely taking place on a smaller scale inside each of us. You have these two different organizations inside of yourself—that part of you that needs to know all the answers, get things done, and have all the data but also that other part of you that really needs to sit back, dream, and understand what's really going on.

If a leader takes the time, he or she can probably accomplish two tasks: personal integration and then some kind of organizational integration. Consequently, a leader is juggling those two components all of the time.

Tom: You said something provocative. You mentioned, "real work," and in my mind that comes from a left-brain perspective. That the real work is crunching the numbers reflects a capitalistic society which measures success with the bottom line. The reality of what I think you're saying is that it really takes the right- and left-brained people within an organization to truly make a company balanced and successful.

Rich: Yes. Most companies over time are pretty good at learning how to make money. In a capitalist society, you either learn how to make money or you are not around. I think that in all the organizations of which I have been a part, financial turnaround has been far more within our grasp than solving the organization's internal problems. Financial turnaround is usually a short-term fix. How do you maintain this over time? How do you deal with the personnel issues that create havoc among your people and impede the work from moving forward over time? When I think about smaller units, like the family, I don't know if more families self-destruct from financial problems or from personal, relational, and social problems. My sense is that if you're not paying attention to both, you're probably going to be in trouble. In the corporate world—in organizational life—the focus isn't generally on the right side of the brain activity, and we just want to call attention to the fact that this is also the real work.

Tom: Rich, you mentioned this turnaround capability that comes into an organization. I would argue that while that might involve a little bit of the right side of the brain, it tends to be a left-sided function because its success is measured financially. The reality, however, is that to become a virtuous organization takes constant work, and this work includes significant right-brain activities. It is constantly repositioning yourself in front of God and your people to build upon virtue. Could you comment on that?

Rich: Typical of an organization might be this scenario. An organization is in financial trouble; capable people are brought in, a strategy is developed, and within two or three years, the organization is feeling financially solid again—it's feeling as though it has a future. But by the time the organization has accomplished a financial turnaround, the culture of the organization has been severely challenged. Now there's another crisis. People have been pushed so hard, have worked such long hours, and have made such great personal sacrifices, that there are, understandably, soaring stress levels.

I remember an organization with which I worked in Boston that had exactly this problem. They had fallen behind their competitors to such a degree that they were wondering whether they could stay in the competitive market. After a three-year turnaround, the culture was so rampant with personnel problems that a significant part of their workforce left. So, virtue integrated with excellence is really the key.

I would just throw this one last question back to you. There's a bottom line mentality in organizations and corporate structures. You've been a leader in that sort of mind-set for twenty-five years. How does a leader, who is responsible for so many other people, maintain his or her own sense of virtue, or in the language of the chapter, how do you keep the right and left brain in some kind of balance?

Tom: I think that is a really good question. I would say that you are quite correct that in industry, even in the not-for-profit industry today, success is measured by numbers and financial outcomes. Even religious-based organizations that talk about mission and have incentives built about mission don't kick in those incentives until the financial goals are met. I know that it has been argued no money, no mission. But, on the other hand, it is really the mission and the service rendered that creates the margin, in my estimation. And for me, no matter what a person's faith tradition is, I find that without prayerful reflection, examination of conscience, and a consideration of the day that was just lived, one cannot be a person of virtue. And only a person of virtue can go out the next day and build an organization of virtue. I do believe leaders lead from the basement of their own darkness. In fact, leaders tend to be in greater darkness than their subordinates, consequently they look out even further because they are so much in the dark. Without, therefore, an examination of conscience it is really impossible to improve. I think that leaders who seek to be virtuous and realize that it takes grace will recognize that there are times when they don't act virtuously, but they have the will, and that will is dominated by the heart. And, if they really have the heart to do it, they can, in fact, change themselves and then—one hopes—lead their organization.

> **Leaders lead from the basement of their own darkness.**

Rich: This is a difficult chapter, and my sense is if there is one chapter readers might ignore, it is this one. It is one of those chapters in which we keep driving home how important it is to make sure that an organization is not stripped of its soul. It is the hardest component to maintain. Every human being has a right- and a left-brain function. We really can't be whole unless we find a way to honor both functions. Organizations are right- and left-brain entities. Until that integration takes place, I don't think that we will ever achieve the goal of elevating the culture of these organizations.

Tom: I agree. In closing, I might add it is interesting that medical schools are finally recognizing that their students need to develop more than just their left-brain capacity. It will be a wonderful day when business schools learn this as well.

Journal Exercise
The Integrated Brain

Look at a situation that is currently on your radar screen. Examine the situation from both the left-brain and right-brain perspectives. Identify both healthy and unhealthy activity based on these two hemispheres. For example:

Left Brain
- Am I being prudent? vs. Am I willing to take a risk?
- Am I respecting the past? vs. Am I dwelling on the past?
- Am I being rational? vs. Am I overanalyzing?
- Am I alert to failure? vs. Am I being afraid to fail?
- Am I being proactive? vs. Am I being reactive?

Right Brain
- Am I taking a risk? vs. Am I being foolish?
- Am I able to accept being wrong? vs. Am I making excuses?
- Am I open to new ideas? vs. Am I being impetuous?
- Am I tapping my intuition? vs. Am I relying too much on feelings?
- Am I acting as a visionary? vs. Am I turning my back on the past?

Spiritual Application
Joy

The deep and substantial state of happiness, called joy, has a primary source for all of us. It usually is accompanied by the feeling of personal peace and meaning. The integration of the brain's two strategies assists the place of joy in a person's life. Wholeness brings joy. Joy finds its expression as a by-product of significant activities and a meaningful life. Joy, unlike pleasure, is not the target itself. We spend a satisfying day with our spouse or our children and end up experiencing a deep and profound joy. Integrating the thinking from both sides of the brain, merging the intellect with the voice of the heart, enables us to be fully human. This is essential in our role as leaders. Only those who live a fully human life will give permission for joy to enter into the workplace. The question is not whether I took pleasure in everything I did today, but did the work I completed and the relationships I entered into bring me joy?

This joy is the result of something. It is more than a feeling—even laughter and the feeling of happiness are of lesser importance. Joy is the result of that which provides our lives with purpose. Virtue is the result of left-brain and right-brain integration. Prudence guides the intellect, moderates the desires, and so on. The soul is whole when we become fully human, functioning on all cylinders. The will, intellect, desires, and emotions living in harmony and submitting to virtue and to each other create the foundation for joy. Deeper than happiness and more profound than pleasure: "I doubt," C. S. Lewis said, "whether anyone who has tasted joy would, ever, if both were in his power, exchange it for all the pleasure in the world."[7]

> **Joy is the result of that which provides our lives with purpose.**

Daily Practice

Read a poem or some devotional material from Scripture. Be aware of your response to the text from both hemispheres. What do you understand from the text from a rational point of view? As you apply reason to the text, what is your response? Give yourself intellectually to this exercise.

Read the text again. What are you feeling? Do you feel any impulse of the heart in relationship to the text? Does the reading have a personal application? Meditate upon the text in your heart.

Take note of integrating these two functions. Always be sure the personal application is not in conflict with the clear meaning of the text.

Chapter Six

Reversing the Binoculars

Leadership Challenge

Jim started an executive coaching practice shortly after leaving a large firm as the director of employee assistance. Within a year the practice was very active. Many of Jim's former colleagues sought private counsel from him. The practice grew more quickly than he had anticipated. The inability to meet the sudden influx of clients became a major problem. Jim had leased an office building with limited space and was locked into a three-year contract.

Expanding the business was going to be difficult unless new office space and partners could be secured. Jim was unprepared to meet this challenge so basic to any business endeavor. He felt a tremendous amount of pressure. Everything seemed to be closing in on him, since he couldn't respond to the increased client load. Since Jim wanted to be a good steward, he decided to step back and take the long view of the situation. He intentionally reversed the binoculars.

Jim thought carefully through his vision. After a time of reflection, Jim felt he had regained perspective. His goals gained clarity. Jim decided to see clients in their office settings. Most executives found this a better option and appreciated the convenience. Jim subleased his existing office space to a new associate who could help him with the overflow. He talked to future clients about his newly organized structure, where they could see a trusted colleague in the privacy of an off-site office or be seen by Jim on-site.

What lesson did Jim apply that brought back the joy of his newfound vocation?

———◆———

Reversing the Binoculars

Do you remember the first time you used a pair of binoculars? There was something magical about viewing a distant object, and then with the assistance of two tubes, seeing that object in close view. Sightseeing was made more exciting and sporting events more intimate. Seeing something up close gave a new perspective.

Likewise, turning the binoculars around created a sense of greater distance of an object. We could now look at something a short distance away, and it would appear far off. This is the dynamic we want leaders to consider during this reflection.

Often, as leaders, we get too close to an issue. We cannot see clearly because our thinking is influenced by a certain subjectivity. We lose the ability to see clearly and are so emotionally involved that the voice of reason is clouded.

Reversing the binoculars can become a discipline that, if practiced, can help us regain perspective. This practice may be viewed as a spiritual discipline, closely related to trust.

> ———◆———
>
> **Often, as leaders, we get too close to an issue.**
>
> ———◆———

In the Sermon on the Mount (Matt. 6:25–34), Jesus teaches us to trust in our heavenly Father. "Therefore I say to you do not be solicitous for your life. . . ." To be solicitous is to be troubled and anxious in mind. It is often the result of the soul and the heart being drawn away from affections of God. We forget who is really in charge and fail to recognize as leaders that we are stewards of all that God has entrusted to us.

When we cannot gain perspective, we forget that God gives life and growth and that our work is a partnership with divine Providence—a partnership that yields to divine wisdom.

Almost every industry has identified leadership as a critical factor for success. A growing number of management experts criticize leadership models, which, they claim, rarely produce the insights organizations need to improve themselves. It is not without reason that leaders become anxious or burdened. Leaders are expected to have the answers. Leaders are paid well to solve problems and to deliver on their promises. Getting distance from a situation can help us remember that God knows our circumstances. Does this matter? Yes. According to Jesus, the one who understands this may rest secure both in prosperity and adversity.[1]

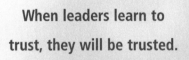

When leaders learn to trust, they will be trusted.

Reversing the binoculars is a practice to gain proper perspective. Every day is a day of trial for the average leader. Demands press in on every side. Not only are leaders expected to produce results, but they must help shape a culture that nurtures a positive attitude toward work and reflects both a creative orientation and a trusting environment, one in which people can work for the love of the work itself or, as Dorothy Sayers says, "for the sake of doing well a thing that is well worth doing."[2]

How can leaders respond to such challenges on their own, regardless of how talented the supporting cast? As the plant springs forth, and could not be without the seed, so every act springs from the hidden seeds of thought, and could not have appeared without them.[3] Leaders who think they can get by on their own intellect and strength are kidding themselves. Jesus says that our Father knows our needs and that confidence must be placed outside ourselves in order to be accessed from within us. Leaders seek trust, but they, too, must learn to trust, especially in wisdom greater than their own. When leaders learn to trust, they will be trusted.

If leaders cannot be trusted or counted on, their presence in an organization is destructive. Without the ability to inspire confidence in others, they lose their effectiveness to lead. To help direct such thinking, leaders should ask themselves the following questions:

- Am I often troubled and anxious about my work?
- Do I have a discipline that enables me to stop and seek perspective?
- Can I follow as well as lead?
- Who do I follow and where is the source of my confidence?
- Is the work I'm involved in promoting the glory of God?

Author Carol Robinson said, "The greed, which characterized the leaders of early capitalism, is now universal and respectable. Americans by the millions take it for granted that all other considerations defer to the profit motive, that everything is to be measured by money."[4] Jesus, however, reminds us of the primacy of spiritual reality. A greater trust in God will not itself rectify things, but it is the prerequisite. By an increase in trust, we mean leaders turning again to God as the end and not a continuation of earthly ends.[5] We believe this is the meaning of Jesus' warning about being solicitous.

Leaders might want to consider two particular constructs in defining their philosophy: servant and steward. The servant conveys the mission and is able to represent it. This is a leader who values honesty, demonstrates trustworthiness, and remains teachable. The servant seeks the highest good of others based on the principle of justice. The steward maintains integrity, shows diligence, honors accountability, and remains faithful to God as the end, which is to be kept in mind and demands our highest loyalty.

Reversing the binoculars can give us the long view of things; it can help us gain perspective and remind us that the view at the top is from a distance. Let those who lead, lead as God directs. It will comfort leaders to remember that the laws of a bad economic system do not bind God, but it will take an heroic faith for the leader to act on this principle.

Reversing the binoculars is a discipline that leaders can use to step back and contemplate the problem. With God's help, the problems we face will teach us what we need to learn and what actions we should take.

Fireside Chat

Rich: Tom, perhaps one of the most difficult challenges for leaders is to gain a certain perspective when you are  under fire. You feel such tremendous pressure as a leader, and so many personal emotions. There are also dissenting voices. It seems there has to be a discipline that allows a leader to think about perspective before perspective is even needed. In your role as a leader, is there any practice or discipline you have maintained over the years that has given you an advantage when you are at one of those moments in your life where you can't see the forest for the trees?

Tom: Yes, there is. You know, power is intoxicating, and it is a little insidious because as a leader you have power of position, if nothing else. What happens is you get deluded sometimes into believing that since you are the leader and you have been imbued with this power, somehow you have this incredible perspective of the organization. Depending on your openness, you may or may not be getting input from others in the organization until, like you said, it is too late.

I have tried a couple of different exercises. I mentioned earlier in previous chapters the need to go humbly in prayer. I find it very helpful to start my day with a meditative perspective and then in the evenings to reflect on the passing day while offering the new day forward.

But I think even more important is the process of discernment as you wrestle with important decisions within the organization and really work with your entire team to ascertain whether or not a particular decision that you are making is consistent with your mission, that you haven't forgotten something, and that you haven't failed to consider other people's perspectives that might be of value. Otherwise, you get deluded by that power, thinking, *Well, I've been successful, I must be, I'm the CEO.* As a result of such thinking, you very quickly become the emperor without clothes.

Rich: How often would you say you are able to touch, using the quote from the end of this chapter, the holy aspirations that you had when you started on this path? How often are you able to capture and frame visually before you, why you wanted to be a leader in the first place?

Tom: I wish I could say it was daily, and maybe part of the therapy of working on this book with you has been reminding myself of one of the reasons why I felt called to leadership. Sometimes you get derailed from the purpose and mission. But I believe that if you apply some of the daily practices that we have discussed it can happen less often. I would say that it would be a luxury to remember your call on a daily basis. I suspect for me it is a lot less than that.

Rich: I'm impressed by organizations that develop what we call learning cultures, but so many of the organizational cultures that I've observed are almost the antithesis of that kind of incubator. Learning cultures allow leaders the ability to be thoughtful, to sit back, to think together with their colleagues, to gain perspective, and to make wise decisions because they're giving some forethought to what they're doing. I'm wondering how we can help change organizations and create at least an awareness that we have to work differently and define our relationships with each other differently. I wonder, is there a way to awaken organizations to the issues of culture, perspective, and virtue.

Tom: I'm going to reverse the binoculars on you and ask you not only that question but even more fundamentally, if you are involved in an organization that has a culture around a very specific mission that includes spirituality, how can you consistently live that out when all of your colleagues, including yourself, are involved in a greater culture that is mediating against success in the spiritual realm?

Rich: And the greater culture being within the organization itself?

Tom: No, outside the organization, extrinsic to the organization. But sometimes maybe it is insidious and creeps in.

Rich: The best way I can answer that is to take personal responsibility. We talk about the personal development of not only leaders but of our colleagues. How do we help people develop consistent cores within themselves? Because it seems to me that the opposition that you are referring to, that fights against the culture that we try to develop in a Christian organization, is the same culture that we are always fighting against in the world personally. How do I help myself and my colleagues enhance our lives through some personal path? In a lot of organizations, and we've been in organizations that deal with these topics, we're starting to pay attention to helping people reach their potential as workers. How do we help them broaden their giftedness? How do we help them see that their contribution is linked to their personhood? I think whether you call it personal formation, personal spiritual

> **We have to actually spend intentional time building up each worker.**

development, or the development of leadership competencies, the question is how do we help people to be further equipped? Whether they are character or skill-based competencies, I think we have to actually spend intentional time building up each worker. And every person in the organization should feel as though the time they take to pay attention to themselves is time they add to the value of the organization. If I take fifteen or twenty minutes for learning purposes, I should not feel that I'm robbing from the organization.

It impressed me once, early in my career as a chaplain, that a physician left the bedside and came back an hour later. The physician explained to the nurse, while I was in the room with the patient, that he really needed to go back to a textbook and gain clarification on an issue that he was addressing. I wondered to myself how many people would have thought that the physician was wasting his time by leaving the room and spending time digesting materials that really would help him with this case. In leadership, if we are seen in an office paging through a book, or reading articles, there is this impression that we are wasting time and not adding value to the work.

Reversing the binoculars is a concept to be used when overwhelmed.

So, in my humble opinion, we need to support each other and encourage each other. It is important for us to be not only excellent in our craft but also continually understanding our work as a calling, a vocation from God. Until organizations give people permission to grow in these ways, we probably aren't going to change the culture. Further, the development of virtue enables leaders to discover within themselves all that was formerly hidden from them—most certainly their shortcomings.

Tom: I think your insights are just tremendous, Rich. An observation that has always perplexed me is why so many people spend so much of their time trying to keep their jobs rather than doing them. But I've gotten a couple of pretty good insights lately. One is that you'll never accomplish all that you want to accomplish in life. That's one thing. Second, you are placed in an organization by God, to do God's work. You're not placed in an organization necessarily to accomplish everything you want. God will call you from that organization if you are not supposed to be there. I think people get confused about that. They think that it is all about them, and it really isn't. It's all about the work that God has called for us. It may be in another place that we're supposed to work out our gifts. So, the organization sometimes isn't the point. It's the work that you are called to do that is the point. God is going to put you where you need to be. The organization is only the place God has you to work out your salvation with him.

Rich: If you lose this perspective, many other objectives get thrown out the window with it. Among them could be virtues as simple as wisdom or prudence. When we are unable to think clearly, perspective is what allows us to step back several times a day. We can ask ourselves some of the questions from the chapter exercises to help see things from a different vantage point from time to time.

Journal Exercise

Reversing the Binoculars

Identify a current situation in your life that is pressing in on you. What is your perspective related to the situation? Reverse the binoculars. Look at the circumstances surrounding this situation from the long view. Ask yourself the following questions:

- What are the pressures of this situation?
- Why are these pressures so profound?
- Is my thinking in this situation a part of a pattern in my life?
- Have I been anxious over other issues lately?
- Are there circumstances that are complicating the issues? If so, what are they?
- Are there moral challenges or ethical issues for me to consider? If so, name them.
- Have I sought advice related to this situation?
- What is the collective wisdom on these issues from my most trusted colleagues?
- Will this situation be important a year from now?
- Can God be trusted to help me with this situation?

With the binoculars reversed, consider one action you can do right now that will help you move this situation toward a desired result. Seek clarity and perspective daily and remember to make choices that advance this situation toward the desirable outcome.

Spiritual Application

Perspective

Our mental outlook defines our perspective, which is the ability to see items in their actual interrelations or comparative importance. Thought and character must, therefore, be closely related. How one chooses to act is guided by one's perspective. We are where we are in our circumstances by the law of our being.[6] A healthy perspective can help the leader make better choices and have a more satisfying arrangement of one's life. Reversing the binoculars is a concept to be used when overwhelmed. "Everyone gets overwhelmed once in a while. That's natural. However, when we have a pattern of being pulled down, we need to change our perspective ... or it will become habitual."[7]

Aristotle taught that we are what we repeatedly do. What we do is guided by thought, so, when overwhelmed, we must step back and give ourselves time to think and consider the situation with clarity. We must meditate and reflect with a desire for divine instruction. We believe Charles Allen was right when he said that "spiritual achievements are the consummation of holy aspirations."[8]

The greatest man is he who chooses right with the most invincible resolution, who resists the sorest temptation from within and without; who bears the heaviest burdens cheerfully; who is calmest in the storms, and most fearless under menaces and frowns; whose reliance on truth, on virtue, and on God is most unfaltering.[9]

One last thought. If our plans are to be successful, we must trust that divine Providence is always at work, thus God's plan for our lives should be sought while perspective helps us conquer our own shortsightedness.

Daily Practice

Sit on a porch or a quiet spot in a park. Have a pair of binoculars handy. Take the time to look at some specific objects using both ends of the binoculars. Reflect on how differently the objects appear based on the perspective. Ponder the choices you have in determining how you will view situations. Reread chapter 1 and chapter 3 on a regular basis.

Decision Making

The price of greatness is responsibility.

Winston S. Churchill

Chapter Seven

The Right
Choice

Leadership Challenge

Jerry perceived himself as a successful chief financial officer, someone respected by his peers, and an advocate for the business of health care. He had been in health-care leadership for thirty years. A competitor that formed a multihospital system throughout the region acquired the health-care facility where Jerry worked. It was Jerry's hope that he could retain his position with the new organization.

Six months after the acquisition, the new company made several significant personnel changes, including dismissing Jerry and four of his peers from the acquired hospital. Jerry had been confronted three months prior to the dismissal with the results of an assessment conducted by his new employer shortly after it purchased his former employer. These results, along with informal assessments by the new company, revealed some significant concerns about Jerry continuing in his role.

Jerry's peers described him as controlling, egocentric, and manipulative. The consensus was clear: it was all about Jerry. Believing this to be a sensitive matter, the new company asked Jerry to meet with a coach who could work through the assessment profile results with him. Jerry refused any suggestions about being coached and demanded that the new organization retract the assessment results, which he termed ridiculous.

Now Jerry was informed that he was being replaced. Jerry refused to leave and threatened a lawsuit. The new company, a faith-based organization, faced a difficult situation. It did not want to be involved in a blood bath. In its own discernment process, the following became clear:

- Jerry's leadership style was unacceptable to the faith-based culture and Jerry had no intention of changing.
- Jerry was given the opportunity to do some remedial work with the new system in the hopes of keeping his career options open with them.
- Refusing help, Jerry was now offered a very just severance package.

The organization spent some time contemplating the problem and confidently followed through with the decision to dismiss Jerry. Did the organization make the right decision?

The Right Choice

Do the thing that is right even when the boss isn't looking because the boss isn't a criterion. The real boss is standing alongside you every moment of your life.
—*Alfred P. Haake*[1]

Choice. Each day we are faced with the seemingly endless opportunity and variability of choice. In a capitalistic society such as ours, choices are legion. Yet how do you decide what is right for you? Not in the trivial decisions but the soulful ones—the ones that can unite me or separate me from God and those around me.

"Can't I do what I like in my life? It's no one else's concern!" This is not just the cry of an adolescent; it is rampant in our society. We think we have a right do as we please.

At a beach sand-building competition, a boy and a girl had finished a magnificent castle and then wandered around to look at the efforts of other children. On returning, they found that another boy had occupied their castle and was adding what he considered to be improvements.

"What are you doing? That's our castle!" they exclaimed.

"No, it's mine. You left it; I found it."

"It's our castle. We made it, and only we can decide what to do with it because we made it."

Of course, everybody said the boy and girl were right; the intruder was turned out, and they won the prize.[2]

The person of faith knows that God is the Creator. God has made us; our life is not our own. God has the right to lay down the conditions of how we must use the life he has given us.[3]

Born with the incredibly wonderful gift of free will, we quickly learn that one man's freedom can be another's straight jacket. Freedom, it turns out, is not altogether free. Since we belong to God, our freedom bears a profound sense of responsibility and is replete with consequences. Each time we exercise our free will, we must be willing to accept the effects of our decisions. In other words, we cannot have both freedom to act and freedom from responsibility.

> Each time we exercise our free will, we must be willing to accept the effects of our decisions.

We will reap what we sow. Before acting, we deliberate; in acting, we choose. Both testify to our freedom. How can we choose correctly? How can we discern God's will for us, even in those smaller decisions that can, when compounded, impact not only our life but also our soul? What are the tools of right discernment that will lead us down the path of righteousness and not destruction? How can we be attentive to the one clear voice within us that illumines the way? The Vincentians (followers of Saint Vincent de Paul) employ a wonderfully helpful tool,[4] not dissimilar to many others used by persons of faith. (It has been modified slightly to fit the text.)

Steps in Discernment

A. Imitation of Jesus Christ
   1. *What criteria would Jesus use?*
   2. *What are the similarities between my motivation and Jesus' motivation?*
   3. *How does this decision help me serve others better?*

B. Unrestrictive Readiness
   1. *Am I willing to look at all choices?*
   2. *Am I willing to let go of control?*
   3. *Am I willing to trust God?*

C. Significance of Events
   1. *What are the significant events?*
   2. *How is God speaking to me through people? Events?*
   3. *Who can give objective input?*

D. The Decision
   1. *Is the decision reasonably clear?*
   2. *Is the decision life-giving?*
   3. *Does this decision made with discernment compel me to action consistent with my faith tradition and own spirit?*

Let's use an example. Overwhelmed with a desire to have a new car, a sporty convertible that I know will make me feel good, I use the discernment model. I quickly go through the first step and arrive at the area of unrestrictive readiness. "Am I willing to let go of control?" Why am I making this purchase, and what are the consequences? Even if I can afford it, is there a consequence to my spirit, my life's energy, that might diminish me? As we consider this rather simplistic example, we can see that even rather mundane decisions carry consequences. Does this mean we can never buy a sports car? Of course not, but rarely does the purchase bring us completion. No thing will complete us; it is our participation in God's intended love for us that does. If we are complete in our spiritual relationship, then the purchase can be enjoyed since we bring joy to the experience rather than expect to extract joy from the experience. This relates to our point in chapter 4 that discernment is understanding and interpreting our viewing point and making an informed decision based on our life view rather than our immediate desires. Included in this life view is the knowledge of God and what he expects of us.

In leadership, a person's ability to properly discern is imperative. Leaders must make decisions consistent with their personal values and the organization's values. Acting dependably and credibly, so that all actions are consistent with these values, is a key to using the discernment model. Leaders must develop that trust, through their decisions, which is the basis for legitimacy.[5] Failure to do so creates a crisis in integrity. Proper discernment and courage can help avoid this crisis.

> **Leaders must make decisions consistent with their personal values and the organization's values.**

Right choices will often require courage. David Cottrell identifies opportunities leaders have to exhibit this courage.[6] We've modified this list slightly:

1. *Have the courage to accept responsibility.*
2. *Have the courage to seek the truth.*
3. *Have the courage to base truth on God's terms.*
4. *Have the courage to take risks.*
5. *Have the courage to stand up for what is right.*
6. *Have the courage to confront the cynics.*
7. *Have the courage to persevere.*

Fireside Chat

Rich: Tom, in the last chapter we talked about perspective. Now we're talking about answering the question "How do you gain perspective?" You've given some attention to a model that you have used over the years. We've both been introduced to

this model in various points of our career—the discernment model. When we discuss discernment, we might scare some people off. But what we're really saying is that without possessing a protocol concerning discernment, we're probably never going to get perspective. How has the discernment model helped you? What has convinced you that it warranted a chapter in this book?

Tom: In the frenetic pace of our lives in this blessed country of ours, we are impetuous in the way we make decisions, in the way we select purchases, and in just about everything we do. Some of our forebearers perhaps had the luxury of stepping back and thinking more carefully. They didn't have all the choices and the challenges we have on a daily basis. I believe that Americans, in particular, make millions of choices and many of them bad, because we don't take the time to step back and apply the collective wisdom that we and others around us have gained about simple things. I used as an example a simple purchase—are you willing to buy this car just because you like it? If you waited thirty days and thought carefully about it, would you be willing to trade off so much of your life's work and energy for this particular purchase? It gets even more important as you make decisions within the context of family, jobs, and experiences in the industry in which you lead. In health care, we are faced with important decisions. For instance, do we equip ourselves in stockpiling medical resources and run up costs for our patients, or do we step back and make more prudent decisions based on a process of discernment that includes a spiritual aspect as well as the realistic components? Can we really afford to do this? Is this really appropriate for the people who are paying the bills? Questions such as these can help us gain perspective.

Rich: In my experience, the busier I was, the more impetuous I had been when making decisions. There is a saying: if you want something done, get a busy person to do it. I have always wondered if the opposite might be true. If you really want to think about something clearly, get a person who has moved away from busyness to help you see what needs to be seen. So, clarity, perspective, and discernment may be the opposite bookend to the activity. We're back to the right- and left-brain functions chapter. I appreciate that we have to accomplish things to be effective leaders. But what we do, as well as how we do it seems, in the long run, to be the signature that we put upon our accomplishments.

Tom: It is. You said something really interesting. Maybe we have to find someone who is not busy to help us get perspective. The early works of Thomas Merton have grown in popularity over the last quarter century. [Note: Merton's later writings and journey toward Eastern thought would not be recommended by the authors.] I suspect the reason for that is because he had time to reflect, and his writings exhibit that sort of thoughtful process.

A currently popular book, that I have only had opportunity to skim through, is called *Father Joe*. It is about the experiences of a fourteen-year-old who is troubled by these issues and is sent to an old Irish monk. It is the recalled wisdom of that Irish monk, long since dead, which still serves this now fifty-year-old in his life as he reflects back to a time that, as a young lad, he received help through many of his challenges. Sometimes we have to do that. I think you hit it right on the head. We do look to busy people to get things done. Sometimes, however, we are just skating the surface of a situation and deep below linger many issues that need to be dealt with. Unfortunately, they are so seldom dealt with in a society as quick, frenetic, and unrelenting as ours.

Rich: If we had taken the time to write a book like this at the beginning of our careers, or at the beginning of our relationship, we may not have had the wisdom to put into it. My sense is that we may have cultivated a certain amount of wisdom that probably would have redefined the way we worked over the years. It is in these moments, when we spend time together, that I see clearly even many of the mistakes that we have made over the years.

Tom: Reflecting on those mistakes, though, and I can think of many myself as we are talking, have they helped or hurt your life of virtue as you have moved forward?

Rich: I'm not sure I understand the question.

Tom: Even though you make mistakes, how do you take those mistakes and create something useful so you can move forward?

Rich: You know, this is one of those questions where I know what I should say, but it is probably more difficult than anything else we have discussed. I think the acknowledgement of a mistake is foremost for any leader or any person. Until we can acknowledge that we have really made mistakes, we cannot learn from them. I don't think most leaders are good at acknowledging their mistakes. However, if we are able to humble ourselves, to cut against our pride, and actually realize and admit that we made a mistake, then the great opportunity for us is that we become vulnerable enough to receive the voices, the messages, and the help that we're normally unable able to hear. More important, there is a concept in the Christian faith that we call grace. It's the kind of concept, both grace and mercy, that we can't experience until we've done something that puts us out of sorts. Then it has this beautiful, refreshing, lovely kind of presence that comes upon us and allows us to see that not only isn't this the worst experience that could have happened but it might be the catalyst that allows us to move forward in the right direction. So, with all my ramblings, I guess I'd say that first I need to acknowledge my mistakes. Then, second, I must realize that making that mistake may actually be the intention that Providence has for me. Unfortunately,

> **Maybe the key is not only in admitting mistakes but in becoming vulnerable.**

one way to do something right is through the trial of having done it incorrectly.

Tom: Rich, I agree with you, yet I am personally challenged. The times that I have become vulnerable and admitted mistakes even within a Catholic organization, I have had those used against me. It didn't feel good that I had admitted those mistakes. But I think if I could focus on the learning that I received, even from just the discomfort, I would perhaps discover even richer truths there than I could imagine.

Rich: I don't know if there is anybody reading those words that won't find some affinity with you in that. Maybe the key is not only in admitting mistakes but in becoming vulnerable because vulnerability places us in a position close to Christ's. Jesus comes and becomes very vulnerable. In a sense, he shows God's hand, he shows God's love, and he shows God's mercy. He forgives the most hardened sinner. He's willing to get down and dirty but then the people say, "Maybe this prophet isn't as strong as we thought; we expected a messiah to come and set up an earthly kingdom." Then they take advantage of him and soon he is humiliated and hanging on a cross. From all appearances, this is a tragedy, but then this great reversal occurs. We find out after the resurrection that it was this very humiliation that served as our medicine. It was the tool that saved us.

I'm wondering when we go through personal humiliation, when we are taken advantage of, if we realize how many people are watching, waiting to see our reactions? I wonder how many people from afar, without our knowing, and maybe we will never know, take solace when they see a leader who doesn't strike back and doesn't give in to pressure but instead stands there and takes it and continues to be a person of virtue.

Tom: Yes, that's the redemptive quality of it.

Journal Exercise
The Right Choice

Pressure from the corporate office to make operating margins is mounting. Company B is in a depressed area, and although it is making a profit, the profit is not large enough to kick in financial incentives for the local CEO, her team, and the national office.

The CEO knows that the only way to hit the huge targets would be an across-the-board force reduction, possibly precipitating an ever-deepening hole for the local economy.

The CEO is local; she grew up in the community, lives there with her family, and would like to stay for a long time. Moments ago, a conversation with her boss went like this, "If you don't do the layoffs and hit your margins, we'll replace you with someone who can." The CEO also knows that the national office may close her division and further sink the region into despair.

Employing a discernment model, enumerate what choices you would make if you were in her position. What is your rationale? Reflect upon your values—what is the greater good? How would you respond?

Spiritual Application
Faith

The object of faith is God.[7] In order to offer leadership which honors spiritual values, one must know God and understand what he has revealed as truth. This describes the virtuous leader. Romano Guardini says virtue denotes something living and beautiful.[8] But it is beauty related to truth. "It is from the eternal goodness of God that moral enlightenment comes into the soul of a person."[9]

Virtue extends through the whole of existence, as a harmony which gathers virtue into unity. And virtue also ascends to God; or rather, it descends from him. Plato already knew this when he bestowed upon God the name of *Agathon*, "the Good."[10]

Faith recognizes the Good as the source of all. Faith would not seek anything but the truth and the right. To do right, to be moral, and to display virtue would be faith's goal. Thus, it recognizes that all truth descends from God.

"Faith is more action than reason. Faith runs ahead of reason. Reason reports, like a camera. Faith takes a stand, like an army. Faith is saying yes to God."[11] Faith, therefore, is demonstrated through obedience. It is doing what is right according to a higher standard. "Not everyone that saith to Me, 'Lord, Lord,' shall enter the kingdom of heaven, but he that doth the will of My Father who is in heaven" (Matt. 7:21). An informed faith compels a leader to live up to the truths that faith proposes. Thus, faith is a master and tutor that teaches us how to live.[12] By faith we regulate the very steps of our lives.

> **An informed faith compels a leader to live up to the truths that faith proposes.**

Daily Practice

Set aside an hour of your time. Sit someplace where you can think. A pencil and paper might be helpful. Consider carefully what criteria you use in making decisions.

Is it congruent with your values and your faith? Are you consistent when using the criteria in decision making? When you make decisions, does God have a place at the table?

Chapter Eight

Not in Kansas
Anymore

Leadership Challenge

XYZ Company had experienced great gains in the past year. It was the seventh straight year of expansion and financial success. The company began with a handful of partners and a small workforce. It had now grown to include two hundred employees and had created a regional presence in the marketplace with five offices. Currently the company was experiencing a plateau effect. Business was steady, but growth had tailed off. A number of partners expressed concern and recommended that the workforce be cut by 10 percent. Other partners disagreed, but the company moved to make the reduction. Many of the remaining employees opted to leave the company rather than become victims of a further downsizing.

The company panicked and closed two of their regional offices. The outcome proved disastrous. Unable to negotiate a time of stabilization, the company moved quickly into a challenging period without a strategic path forward. Workers at the XYZ Company became increasingly resistant to the company's response, and a significant morale problem surfaced within the company's culture. Employees were never consulted, and a certain grudging compliance replaced what was once commitment from the team of workers.

The company created a self-fulfilling prophecy. If change had been properly analyzed, the company might have responded to the plateau effect with an understanding that this was part of a normal cycle. Their decision toward under-investment through a workforce reduction accelerated the crisis with little time for thoughtful response. Now the company had to make difficult decisions about how to encourage the culture to regain confidence.

Is all lost? How can the company regain its potential?

Not in Kansas Anymore

All of us remember the scene from *The Wizard of Oz* when Dorothy, sensing that Oz was very different from where she came, exclaims to Toto, "We're not in Kansas anymore." Whenever we recognize that life's circumstances have changed, we realize that we are no longer in Kansas. As leaders, we must be committed to see with new eyes and learn to be successful in a world different from the one we have known. This means change. Leaders must determine future steps while identifying the current reality, as well as the obstacles and impediments to the vision.

Change requires leaders to skillfully and enthusiastically steer the organization to both think and work differently. It means that leaders will be called to face problems, address challenges, and resolve creative tensions to reach the desired vision. Any activity we initiate to help modify our thoughts, feelings, or behavior is a change process. Resolving creative tension, therefore, is the art of negotiating the challenges of change toward the realization of our desired result.

Commitment to change is a decision to challenge any current circumstances that are in need of transformation. It is the acknowledgement that we are no longer in Kansas. Leaders must accept the reality of change when change proves necessary. This requires us to both recognize and experience the difficulties of change. We must realize that strong emotions are an essential part of the process. Developing fresh mental models, additional competencies, and new coping skills will be necessary to a leader's strategy.

Natural law teaches us many truths about change. Through the seasons, for example, we learn that there are cycles that govern the world in which we live. That it is cold in the middle of winter should not surprise us, since it is intrinsic to the season. That it is hot and often uncomfortable during some summer periods is something most of us expect. The spring will bring flowers and the autumn falling leaves. We have experienced the cycles before and recognize such trends. Scripture itself is clear that there is a time and a season for everything. For all people, for all organizations, for all movements, there are inevitable challenges and changes that occur. They may challenge both our viewing point and our point of view.

Change often brings the responsibility to determine a proper course of action. Initially there may be the uncomfortable reality of denial, resistance, and confusion on the parts of those who want to hold on to what was. During a time of challenge or crisis, leaders must help associates work through their initial responses and move toward discernment and decision.

Discernment is when we seek to understand and even explore the new if it proves to be prudent. Here, leaders must be open to methods that will respond to the needs of the time and promote improvement that is both neces-

This requires us to both recognize and experience the difficulties of change.

sary and virtuous. When change seems necessary, we must make sure that it is good. This is not easy to determine—especially when change for change's sake often appears to be a solution. On the other hand, we may be emotionally tied to what is and not want to explore the possibilities of change, even for the good.

When people are struggling with change, denial, resistance, and confusion are not usually permanent responses. They are responses, however, that can indicate either a necessary roadblock to a bad idea or real evidence of how difficult it is for us to explore new ways of thinking, acting, and being. If we can help people analyze and discern, then the best decisions can be made about moving forward.

During the season of choices, leaders may need to consider the following thoughts. We must determine how to meet challenges. Do we need to move in a new direction? If not, what course of action should be taken? Why is the current reality being threatened? How has this happened? Can we find real value and meaning in committing to a new direction? Is change desirable and/or necessary?

Commit to recognize and celebrate successful change efforts.

Sometimes challenges are forced upon us by a paradigm shift. Here, new thinking emerges and questions old methods before they actually become obsolete. Discernment is absolutely necessary because the challenges affect our actions as well as our thoughts. To change may contradict long-standing strategies. It must be noted here that discernment may require leaders to question the notion that all change is good. It should also encourage us to ensure that necessary changes become good. Again, we recognize the need for reason and objective truth reflecting the pattern of God's wisdom: seeing from the highest perspective the relationships that exist among things, giving meaning and measure to that which does change.[1]

Consider the following checklist to ensure that necessary change becomes good:

- Take time to thoroughly plan for changes.
- Give a sound reason for any changes that are to be made.
- Be specific about the goals, purposes, and potential benefits of change efforts and communicate them to everyone in the organization.
- Give the organization a very clear definition of how success will be measured.

- Be sure that those responsible for overseeing the change implementation are skilled thinkers and listeners.
- See to it that the employees who are affected by a change take part in the planning and implementation of that change, whether or not they were involved in the change decision.
- Spend time learning from any recent efforts at change that did not succeed and find out the reason for the lack of success.
- Assist those who have problems implementing changes by communicating freely with them and asking for their help.
- Encourage the organization to accept responsibility in moving forward and to refrain from blame.
- Commit to recognize and celebrate successful change efforts.
- Offer training to employees for coping with change.
- Give voice to the organization's excitement about what the future holds.

Fireside Chat

Tom: Rich, a lot of your work has been in the area of change and change management. I find this chapter especially

provocative. I see, as I look around me, a massive shift in what is happening in the world as we know it. It is happening in our churches. It is happening within our country. I am anxious to hear from you.

Rich: Seeking God gives that perspective and wisdom. I have probably given as much thought to change as to any of the tools and the philosophies concerning organizational theory that we have discussed. I have this profound sense that change is a spiritual concept that God uses to remind us over and over again that we're not in charge. I believe God uses it to test us as well. The difficulty of change demands a mature and discerning mind. Often we are resistant to change and the challenges it brings because we want to live life on our terms. Over the years I have noticed that people rarely get angry unless life doesn't go the way they want it to go. Change signifies that life is taking us in a direction that reveals that we are not sovereign, which probably accounts for our denial of and resistance to it. One important issue related to change is how we learn to accept the fact that it is ongoing. I remember an experience from childhood, when my mother switched a favorite drinking glass of mine and gave it to a neighbor at a dinner party. I never realized that the disappointment I felt at that moment was just the first of many as situations would not always be the way I wanted them to be. So, part of this chapter addresses the critical relationship between change and life on one's own terms. This might be the chapter where we ask leaders to grow up and accept the fact that if we are going to mature as leaders, we are going to have to help people change, and we ourselves are going to have to endure the white waters of change. One caution, however, is that not all change is good. Some changes actually undermine our human dignity. We can discuss this later.

> Not all change is good. Some changes actually undermine our human dignity.

Tom: I've heard it said that there is a fifth Gospel, and it is what the Holy Spirit is writing within us. The Spirit working through our own lives, transforming us into God's image.

Rich: That's a beautiful picture.

Tom: I think with change sometimes we have to discern the Spirit moving through us and understand what we are to do. As you mentioned, not all change is good.

As you think back on your career and the many difficult situations you've encountered, what is the most
challenging one you have had? And, can you tell us
briefly how you approached it?

Rich: Counterintuitively, change has always been more difficult for me when I initiated it. Part of that is because I
feel personally responsible for the decision and the
results. When I have to live with the consequences, I
am living with consequences that resulted from my
own free will. On the other hand, when a decision is
thrust upon me, like a change in documenting patient
activity for reimbursement purposes, I may feel a
certain frustration, but in the end I try to accept it and
make the best of the situation.

Going back to your original question, one of the most
difficult changes I made, as you are aware, happened
some twenty years ago when I left the ministry of the
United Methodist Church. I made that change at a time
when I loved what I was doing. There was even something about my identity as a minister that I loved. But
there was no longer an internal conviction for my
actions. I came to believe there was a greater Christian
truth and, as you know, I became a Catholic. This
change involved both a personal decision and a call
beyond my control. We identify it as grace. God was
working within me, and I had a decision to make. So, I
was challenged to live according to the dictates of
integrity, that is, congruency between what I say and
what I do. I had to align myself with what I really
believed. In so doing, people felt confused. My congregation could not understand. This marked a pivotal
time in my life. It helped me understand that forces are
at work beyond ourselves all the time, and we must
respond to them with wisdom and discernment.

Some forces and influences are good, and some are
not. That is why I am not a person who simply says

that change is good. It can be, but sometimes change is the result of misreading a situation or not understanding yourself or your circumstances. I have accepted some changes that I didn't think were best (like a tax increase), but I have certainly resisted change when I thought it was destructive (like innovations in the Mass or Sacred Liturgy). Some change is absurd from a Christian point of view. How can you, for example, alter revelation? You can't improve on the Commandments or the Beatitudes because they are of divine origin.

Now I will throw the question back to you. Many times when we make changes in organizational life, it appears to be the admission that we were doing something wrong, which it may be. But, in most cases change is a necessary next step. Given the accelerated pace of organizational life, the only way to stay up with an industry is to improve processes, which often means change. So, how do you become that person who owns up to or initiates change in environments where people often see that as an admission that all is not going well? How do you keep the perception moving in the right direction while you're changing the landscape?

Tom: One key to that is education, and I'll explain why. Research shows that 95 percent of the companies that start in America fail in the first five years or so. In order to be successful they have to be adaptable. They might not have had to change that quickly in the Middle Ages, but today the world changes rapidly. There is a sense of immediacy and finality because of weapons of mass destruction and the like that we have in the modern world. The pace of information and our ability to obtain it is staggering. Leaders, in addition to using discernment, have to continually educate members of their team about what is happening so there is an understanding of the internal and external environments. Even if some alteration seems a little precipitous, no one is shocked that change is taking place because they know that the success of the organization is the ability to adapt.

I think the other key is empowerment. Issues concerning integrity and virtue should come from the top down, but ideas can come from the bottom up. Leaders have to create flexibility within the organization. While the mission should not change, it may need to be fulfilled according to a different strategy. An organization has to trust its leader, and its leader has to be honest and forthright about issues, take responsibility for mistakes, and commend others for success. I think that creates a culture that forgives mistakes, celebrates success, and has the adaptability and flexibility to progress despite tough decisions.

Rich: If there is one issue that I would address differently in my own career concerning change, it would be to discuss the changes with the people who are affected by them in order to give them hope and a means to still be successful in light of the changes. I think we often ask people to shift gears in life needlessly. We expect people to make these uncomfortable changes, but we don't answer the questions that they are most interested in. Specifically, *What does this mean for me?*

In health care, when nurses are forced to spend so much time away from what they love to do because they are now required to document patient charts and address new regulations, we have to ask if this makes sense. How can we help caregivers feel good again about what they are doing? This is the challenge of change.

Tom: I think we need to remember that although we may be the leader in an organization, we're really there to serve these wonderful people whose responsibility it is to carry on its work. So, if as a servant-leader we respect every member of our team, we'll approach change differently. We'll recognize that first they need to know that it is okay; the result from this change will be positive. We need to move in this direction, but we will find a right way to do it. Let creativity come from them. Recognize the profound responsibility that we have as leaders. People are looking to us for the answers, and sometimes we just don't have them. Having a deep respect for the people whom we are called to serve means recognizing that they are not at our beck and call. It is actually the opposite. We're there to be at their beck and call to determine how we can best iron out the wrinkles in the organization.

> Good judgment includes our ability to count the cost.

Rich: Tom, in ending this chapter, I want to recognize that there are some changes organizations make that aren't across the board or universally good for everybody. There are some changes that result from difficult decisions. It may even cost a person his or her job. This is where the rubber meets the road for leaders because we sometimes have to make decisions that appear to strip the dignity from people. When we have to make changes that are that profound and affect people's careers and their income—well, that's maybe a leadership question that is yet to be answered. How do we remain noble at a time when the decisions we are making appear to be ignoble?

Tom: That's a profound question. No leader I know enjoys making those decisions nor enacting them. I have found in my career that the most difficult task I have to do is to sit down with somebody, who is dependent upon my organization for his or her income and well-being, and separate them from the company. Even if the person has made poor choices, we still need to approach the situation with compassion. I don't know how to best answer the question other than to encourage us to approach the person with profound respect. Really, that's how we have to deal with this difficult situation. We have to say to ourselves, *If I had to approach my God, what would I say in this situation that would ensure the dignity of this particular separation?*

Rich: I'd say this could lead us toward a larger conversation. It does mean, however, that exit strategies must reflect a willingness to provide for people a just separation. This becomes a very important human resource function.

Journal Exercise

Not in Kansas Anymore

- Define briefly your personal philosophy of change. Is all change for the good?
- What are your most difficult challenges when you are faced with changes in your life?
- What have you learned about yourself as a result of making necessary changes?
- How do the decisions we make during a time of challenge and change help us grow?

Final Thought: Contemplate your current reality during times of challenge. Consider carefully future decisions. Remember that change is not always the answer.

Spiritual Application

Good Judgment

Good judgment requires that we understand and see clearly the issues at hand. There is a connection among good judgment, wisdom, prudence, and wise counsel. Jesus taught that good judgment includes our ability to count the cost before moving too quickly on a project. This holds true for an opinion as well. Scripture indicates the need to "go up to the mountain of the Lord . . . and he will teach us his ways" (Isa. 2:2).

Good judgment is important to the discussion on change. The ability to make a sound decision requires truth and clarity. Bob Wicks says:

> That with clarity, our actions become psychologically sound and spiritually responsive. Yet most of us consciously or unconsciously avoid seeing the Light. This may sound ridiculous, since being clear is so akin to being fully aware, fully alive. However, the process involved in seeing life clearly requires a good deal of focused energy and often forces us to give up many of our nostalgic illusions.[2]

He maintains, "Seeking to be clear is the only real journey."[3] Clarity will then be a major influence upon good judgment since the specific goal of clarity is achieving perspective.[4] Perspective has everything to do with our viewing point and its ability to picture situations as they really are. Defects in this area include thoughtlessness, rashness, negligence, indecisiveness, and inconstancy in execution.[5]

Common sense, humility, and docility all assist good judgment "to discern in every circumstance, our true good and to choose the right means for achieving it."[6]

Daily Practice

Think about the changes you want to make in your own life. Which changes are necessary for your own personal growth? What would you need to do today that would contribute toward your desired goal?

If our plans are to be successful, we must make good judgments about our course of action and trust that divine Providence is always at work. Decide how you would cooperate with God's plan for your life. Clarity will help you conquer your own shortsightedness.

Chapter Nine

The People We Love To Be With

Leadership Challenge

Melody was four months into her role as the CEO of a community-based hospital. She had inherited a team that had served with the former CEO for four years. Having moved from a significant geographical distance, it was difficult for her to identify where her support system was and whom she could trust. Melody was just beginning to learn about her team both professionally and socially. It was a team that traditionally worked and played together, involving members of their families in social activities.

One thing that bothered her was the consistent thread of gossip that ran through the team. Melody was becoming aware of who the catalysts were for the team's consistent movement in this direction. She believed that a person's character was the complete sum of all their thoughts, and this proclivity toward gossip was not only counterproductive to the work environment but revealed the true substance of a person's heart.

Especially disturbing was that the persons most responsible were in pivotal senior leadership positions. Social gatherings were a time for some team members to reveal company secrets involving the workers that reported to them. Melody decided to dismantle the old gang and build a new team. Too much water under the dam and too much game playing convinced her she needed to move to a totally new space. Melody wanted leaders with solid character with whom she could consult on confidential matters and to whom the hospital employees could look to as role models for the organization. Melody was clear about the people she wanted to keep in the organization she had been entrusted to lead. What are her next steps, and how should Melody carry them out?

The People We Love To Be With

What a strange topic for a chapter on leadership. Yet we believe this topic to be of special significance. We intend, therefore, to raise a most important question. How can we really find happiness in a life where there is so little truth, so little faith, so little loyalty; where malice and ambition rule; where virtue is neglected and forgotten; where money means everything and a son sometimes desires the death of his own father in order to come into the inheritance?[1] Some may escape the vale of tears experienced by the masses, yet even here, our earthly happiness cannot last any longer than our lives.[2]

Happiness, or beatitude, is a universal quest. Yet, this state we seek is impossible without knowledge of our ultimate end or true purpose in this life. This purpose has to do with our immortal souls. We cannot be excused for knowing nothing about the happiness of the next life and must see this life in light of eternity. Our creator recognizes our soul's need for friendship and communion. Indeed, in Christ he comes, redeems us, and invites us to be his friends. Consider our Lord's elevation of the apostles: "I will not now call you servants: for the servant knoweth not what his Lord doth. But I have called you friends . . ." (John 15:15). Earlier he had said to them, "Greater love than this no man hath. That a man lay down his life for his friends" (John 15:13).

A leader must not only be surrounded with loyal, like-minded people in the workplace but must nurture friendships that will sustain the soul over the course of a lifetime. The book of Proverbs says, "He that is a friend loveth at all times" (17:17). A true friend, that is, a spiritual friend, is one with whom we have no secrets. He is also one who will lay down his life for us, as our Lord did, describing this act of supreme love as an act of friendship.[3] Having people like this in one's life is a blessing but does not happen without effort. Relationships of such substance are defined by charity and commitment. Often, it will take a lifetime to cultivate even a handful of such friendships in our lives. The point is, however, that we must seek this with the same passion with which we seek after a career.

Aelred of Rievaulx, a twelfth-century Saxon monk and Cistercian abbot, says that God, whose own friendship to his creation is manifested throughout nature, implants the impulse to friendship in man. He describes our affinity for friendship as human nature's expression of that "vestige of unity from him who is supremely and purely one."[4]

Loving God and loving our neighbor go hand in hand. Friendship is the highest manifestation of the love we have toward our neighbor because it most closely resembles our soul's love for God. Consider for a moment our desire to obey God and to be congruent with his views. We desire his ways to become our ways. So, too, spiritual friendship reflects common themes about what is important. In fact, Aelred explains how one should withdrawal from a friendship that offers

> A leader must nurture friendships that will sustain the soul.

no possibility of becoming a spiritual one. For how could we be in full union with someone who fundamentally shares different views about essential matters? We could certainly stand by a friend who falls and expresses sorrow, but could we be joined with a personal friend who felt the marriage vow is not to be honored and blatantly disregarded his or her duties? This would not reflect the nature of divine love. Lines must be drawn. We must, however, always maintain a high regard for the former friend in light of the love we once felt for them.[5] This is true charity, for even when lacking in affinity and affection, we still love our neighbor and seek that neighbor's highest good. That reflects God's love, who sends the rain to sustain both the righteous and the unrighteous. What greater praise could be given to any virtue?[6]

Spiritual friendship is the reflection of divine intimacy that seeks to have all things in common. Cicero's definition in his treatise *On Friendship* states: "Friendship is agreement on both human and divine affairs, combined with goodwill and mutual esteem."[7] As such, "spiritual friendship is the only lasting friendship, because it alone accords with our true purpose in life: the consecration of our wills to God. Aelred sees human friendship as a form of mediation by which we ascend toward divine love."[8] As leaders, our private lives must be nourished to support the virtue necessary for our roles. Aristotle listed *ethos* at the top of his qualities for leadership. The ethos is a leader's moral character and the source of his ability to convince others.[9] Spiritual friendship is essential to the development of moral character, as our thoughts and behaviors reveal the influences of our lives.

> The people we love to be with ought to reflect the pulse of our moral character.

"Tell me thy company and I'll tell thee what thou art." These words from the famous book, *Don Quixote de la Mancha* by Miguel de Cervantes, hit the mark. The people we love to be with ought to reflect the pulse of our moral character. And, when we are back at the office faced with the challenges and difficulties of leadership, our performance should be a reflection of with whom we spend time on the human and the divine levels.

We could all learn from these words: "Son, observe the time, and fly from evil. For thy soul be not ashamed to say the truth. For there is a shame that bringeth sin, and there is a shame that bringeth glory and grace. Accept no person against thy own person, nor against thy soul a lie. Reverence not thy neighbor in his fall" (Eccl. 4:23–24).

Fireside Chat

Tom: Rich, this is a really unusual chapter to include in a book on leadership. There's a quote from Proverbs that says,  "He that walketh with the wise, shall be wise: a friend of fools shall become like to them" (Prov. 13:20). Could you comment on why we selected this topic for the chapter? I think it is very provocative.

Rich: One of the ideas we have discussed concerning the kind of leadership model that we value is that a lot of decisions that we make as leaders are collective wisdom decisions. Very few leaders act alone anymore, and when you are looking for collective wisdom, you're really trying to honor the team you have chosen. However, if you aren't surrounded by the right people, then it makes it very difficult to make decisions that are virtuous and value based. Those with whom you surround yourself will define your own character over time.

Given your long career in leadership, maybe I can throw the question back to you. If, in fact, those with whom we associate really reflect our own character and ultimately have great bearing on the virtue of our decisions, what considerations should be made in selecting leader colleagues? Have you had experiences in your own life in which your associates made a difference in terms of your own personal success?

Tom: The people I've worked with have always made a difference in my own personal success or lack thereof. So, the selection of your leadership team is not only critical but is probably the most important decision you make in your career. Those relationships have to go deeper than the average friendships we have in western society. They must be deep, spiritual friendships. Your friends should be people who care about you, not only physically and for your success within the context of the organization, but also your decisions as they relate to your own salvation and your relationship with God. Consequently, if you make bad selections and choose people whose desire for you is less than good, you will not only be diminished as a leader but you will create chaos within the organization.

Rich: Certainly, a very frequent model in the world is for a CEO or a leader to hire the people he perceives to be the most competent. But it might not be the norm for leaders to pursue the most virtuous or value-based people. I've been in organizations where people hire their friends, but it's not because their friends are virtuous or competent. At the same time, we have in corporate America today a crisis around character. So, I think this chapter has much relevance given the current reality of where we are in our culture.

Tom: I quite agree. In our American corporate culture today, how many of your colleagues are willing to lay down their lives for you? It seems to me that many are more worried about keeping their jobs instead of doing them. Or, perhaps they are more worried about their own personal advancement than the mission of the organization.

Rich: I really think we have to be honest about what lives inside of us. When we say we love and care for our families, especially with financial care, there is often something selfish in it for us. It really means that we want our families to be launched into some sort of upper social sphere. We need to be better at calling America and leaders back to their souls. Instead of talking about work as a profession, we need to refer to it as a vocation. We need to discern whether we are driven to do something, or are called by God to respond to something, that takes us beyond ourselves. Perhaps as leaders, our real work is to help people focus on what they're really supposed to be doing. What provides meaning? What provides value? And, what, in a larger sense, helps us respond to a calling?

Tom: You know, Rich, I reflect on my father, who was a prominent business leader but got a neurological disease at the height of his power and prestige. He was a very spiritual man. He suffered for over ten years with this disease and still died fairly young. What amazed me was how, after ten years, few of his associates were present during his illness or at his funeral. It just struck me that so much of this power with organizations is ephemeral. You really do have to find those intimate, spiritual friendships that sustain you. That's what it's all about. You made a compelling statement earlier that people are concerned about taking care of their families and their financial security. But, is taking care of the family really about economic success only? I wonder what would happen if we realized that substituting character for economic success was really at the destruction of our own souls and our very reason for being?

> **How many of your colleagues are willing to lay down their lives for you?**

Rich: One final point. Maybe the most provoking question in a chapter like this urges leaders to ask themselves, when hiring processes take place, *Why do I want this person working beside me?*

Tom: Great question.

Rich: It is an important question, and one that takes us back to the purpose of writing this chapter. We have said that loving God and loving our neighbor go hand in hand, and that friendship is the highest manifestation of the love we have toward our neighbor because it most closely resembles our soul's love for God. This being the case, our decisions about coworkers are important in light of our love for God. If we really love God more than we love ourselves (not characteristic of the natural man since the fall), we must honor relationships in ways that are pleasing to him. One way to do this is to seek out other leaders whose values and core beliefs reflect a certain growth in charity and a desire to do all for the glory of God. This will not be popular in today's world. By current standards, it may even sound discriminatory. But a higher standard will call us not to turn our backs on heavenly principles. Bottom line: I want people working beside me who will love their neighbors (and thus their coworkers) as themselves.

Journal Exercise

The People We Love to Be With

Carefully think through and list the criteria that make for collegial success at the leadership level. For example, "it is important to me that my colleagues in leadership are people who value (create your list):"

Here's our short list:
- Self-knowledge
- Self-discipline
- Prudence
- Justice
- Temperance
- Fortitude
- Hope
- Love of neighbor
- Faithfulness
- A cultivated spiritual life
- Patience
- Integrity
- Accountability
- Perseverance

Spiritual Application
Diligence

"I am the vine, you the branches . . . for without me you can do nothing" (John 15:5).

We need to heed the company we keep. We must be in earnest about making the right decisions and persistent in our application of this undertaking. A leader's life is shaped by such decisions. This is especially true in our relationships.

Have you ever considered not making relationship decisions alone? Have you ever considered the possibility of making better decisions *with* God? Scripture actually encourages this course of action. "Come and let us go up to the mountain of the Lord . . . and he will teach us his ways" (Isa. 2:2). Think about it—stepping out and making decisions with the One who guides and shapes the course of all events. Perhaps the most important element in decision making *is* to invite God into the process. The people we love to be with ought to also receive guidance from the One who knows the way. Together we can become the people through whom God's work is accomplished.

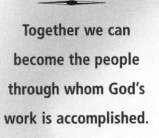

Together we can become the people through whom God's work is accomplished.

Scripture poses the question: "What fellowship does light have with darkness?" The spiritual friendship we have been discussing and to which God calls us is rare in our day.

We need friends, however, and we often settle for less than the ideal. The danger in such compromise is that we imperil the integrity of our religious vision when we exempt from it certain relationships that can find no footing on the ground of our faith. But just as a man

*cannot serve two masters, neither can a friendship. Other
people draw us toward God, or they lead us away.*[10]

Daily Practice

Contemplate these words everyday:
He that walketh with the wise,
shall be wise: a friend of fools
shall become like to them.

Proverbs 13:20

Solitude

*Now you are no longer caught
in the obsession with darkness,
and a desire for higher love-making
sweeps you upward.*

Johann Wolfgang von Goethe

Chapter Ten

The Hidden
Voice

Leadership Challenge

Paul was faced with a difficult decision. A colleague, Joe, was being considered for a significant leadership role in another part of the country but within the same industry. Joe had recently received some less-than-favorable comments on recent performance appraisals, including some challenges by other colleagues who completed a 360-degree peer review.

Joe approached Paul to give a recommendation by phone since Paul was an executive vice president of the current organization. Paul was asked to be supportive. Joe assumed that he would comply without any problem. Paul asked Joe when the company might call him for the recommendation and told his colleague he would touch base with him the next day.

That night Paul spent some quiet time alone. He wrestled with his conscience as to whether he could give a good recommendation. Paul had experienced several firsthand examples of Joe's lack of accountability and thought he would be misleading the other company. Furthermore, Paul had been considering probation for this same coworker. To further complicate the matter, Joe was a personal friend. In solitude the answer came.

The next day Paul called his colleague-friend into his office and told him the truth—he could not give the kind of recommendation his friend was looking for. Paul was, however, willing to coach Joe and set him on the right course so that a future reference would be possible.

Did Paul respond appropriately? Did he listen to the right voice during moments of solitude?

The Hidden Voice

Leaders often find themselves in a dark wood. As Dante relates to us in the *Divine Comedy*, "In the middle of the road of my life I awoke in a dark wood where the true way was truly lost."[1] It is here that the true leader must face the dark side and then find self. There is, deep within each person, a hidden wellspring. It is there that one finds the union with God, and, when dug deeply enough, the well will not run dry. This is where the leader, in the dark times, must turn.

As we look at leaders, we often perceive them as extraordinarily fortunate, people to be envied and whose lives are laudable and desirable. Unless we have held such a position, few of us understand the time they have spent in the desert or the time in the deep dark wood where all seems forbidden and lost. Poets have written about it, hermits have prayed about it, and leaders have lived through it. Yet it is in the darkness that we often find the hidden voice within ourselves. That hidden voice is a voice of moral courage, of solitude and contentment, of reflection and gratitude, and can only be the voice of God. Yet, we encounter so much noise: the droning input from meeting after meeting, the criticisms of our boards of directors, clashing of our colleagues, and and the complaints of our subordinates. There are newspapers with their opinions, stockholders with their demands, consumers with their needs, workers' families with their hopes. All of these must be dealt with.

Without the ability to reflect as St. Francis of Assisi did before the cross in San Damiano, the leader can be overwhelmed by the demands and expectations of the many. Francis said, "Most high, glorious God, enlighten the darkness of my heart and give me, Lord, a correct faith, a certain hope, a perfect charity, sense and knowledge so that I may carry out your holy and true command."[2] This prayer of Francis reminds us that each of us has a time of darkness in the heart which is our call to prayer that can connect us with our God. True leaders who are in touch with their souls will dig deeply and prayerfully, and seek, in these times of confusion, an input greater than they can comprehend. They will seek the hidden voice within and because their prayerful aspect is in continual dialogue with God, the leaders can be confident that the hidden voice is truly God speaking to them.

Leaders need to listen to that inner voice and recognize that it is Providence that put them in such circumstances, and Providence will provide. But trusting in Providence requires a confidence and moral courage that comes from placing one's self before God on a regular basis. The confidence comes from knowing the other person, God; relationships are not built overnight but over time. Because we responded "yes" to God in leadership, God will not let us down. God will respond in an unqualified "yes" as he did to us upon the cross. The cross of leadership then reflects the leader's participation in the event on Calvary. It is there that the Leader of heaven and earth forever reconciled us with the Father, and so it is there that leaders finds their true selves, because it is in dying to themselves that they are free to ultimately lead.

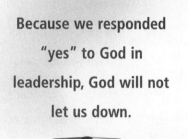

Because we responded "yes" to God in leadership, God will not let us down.

What an incredible mystery it is that in dying to one's self completely the true nature of leadership can ultimately be found. It is so contrary to the common understanding of what leadership is, yet so consistent with God's expectations of us. Leaders are fully human. Tainted with the sin that expelled us from Paradise, our pride can lead us to delusion that believes our leadership is something entirely constructed by our own will and confidence. We somehow perceive that our personal vision and charisma help us prevail. Unless that vision is tempered by God's will, discerned by recognizing the one clear voice deep within us, and unless that charisma, truly a gift from God, is used to clarify that vision, the leader will not succeed. Perhaps for a short time the leader will enjoy success as defined by this world, but the true evidence of success is the survivability of that vision to the next generation.

After leaving an organization, can we claim that future generations will enjoy the fruits of our vision because it was consistent with God's will, or will, in fact, our leadership be burned on the funeral pyre of history, as forgotten as Ozymandias' lying face down in the desert?

Reflect back to the chapters on discernment, personal integrity, and decision making. Part of leadership is to be both out in front of the world and then to retreat from it. It is here in this retreat, in the solitude of sitting with the great Master, that we can hear the true mandates of leadership: "Blessed are the peacemakers . . . Blessed are the poor in spirit." It is here, at the foot of the Master, that we open up to the true mystery and richness that this responsibility brings. The leader has been given an incredible gift from God, a share in Calvary. With this cross, the leader is also offered the opportunity for contemplation, to be still before God. In that stillness, in the quiet dawn of our understanding, the one voice emanates as a quiet groan and completely becomes the depth of our longing—the voice of God. When we as leaders listen to this voice, we are free to lead and, in that experience, find our own salvation. Listening to God allows him, by means of his gifts, to govern, strengthen, and sustain us in our spiritual lives.

> Listening to God allows him, by means of his gifts, to govern, strengthen, and sustain us in our spiritual lives.

When we listen to God, "the gift of counsel teaches, advises, and directs us so that we may diligently put into effect those things which we prudently judge to be the most conducive to our salvation and the greater glory of God."[3] Leaders will find it difficult to practice virtue without God's assistance. The grace of God, "by the virtues and holy habits it produces, cures our ills, heals our wounds, enlightens our intellect, inflames our will, strengthens our weakness, pacifies our passions, rectifies our evil inclinations, restores our taste for spiritual things, gives us distaste for carnal things, and makes the yoke of God's law sweet."[4]

Fireside Chat

Rich: We discussed the people that we love to be with, and we referred to Aelred's writings in terms of his under-

standing of friendships and how to cultivate friendships in the workplace. We're going a step further, really down to the structural level. We're talking about the leader's ability to nurture silence, to listen, to hear God's voice, to have their consciences formed by something that is deeper than themselves. So we're not trying to hide, if we ever did, the fact that this is a book for leaders who are interested in a spiritual frame of reference. How would you respond if someone were to say to you, "Tom, why write a book that highlights leadership from a spiritual frame of reference and especially a chapter like this that deals with cultivating a relationship with God to give a spiritual frame of reference?"

Tom: I would say that when embarking upon a leadership role, you are completely unaware of what you are getting yourself into. And it is through the dark night of the soul, or as Francis discovered in the darkness, that you encounter a long and lonely road unless you are really focused on God. It is in the experience of that darkness that you truly get to see the dawning of the light, in your relationship with God. The temptations in leadership, because of power and wealth and all that goes with it, are profound. A leader can easily lose his or her way. Your friend, Bob Wicks, describes leaders as so often being in the great darkness of the basement. One of the reasons they cast a broader light is because they are so deep in the darkness; they are much more in the darkness than everyone they are leading. That's a cause for deep and important reflection, and I think that leaders who do not discover their own weakness, nor realize their dependence on and relationship to God will never find their way. They may be considered good leaders, but their fruit will come to nothing.

Rich: If you look at what happened to the nation of Israel in the Old Testament, you will recall a time when almost all of their neighbors had a king. They all had monarchies and leaders they could point to. Israel became jealous of their neighbors because they had visible kings. They petitioned God for their own king. God didn't will it, but they wanted it. And they wanted it so much that they ended up believing that God willed it. It's probably what can happen to all of us in leadership. We go after something because we desire it. And we desire it for so long, without any type of process check, either with good spiritual friends or in that silence in the darkness, that we begin to believe that God wills it for us. I know, personally, that I always fear that dynamic in my own life. In some ways, our friendship has been a system of checks and balances for me.

> Leaders that do not realize their own dependence on and relationship to God will never find their way.

Tom: Yes, it's interesting. In a piece I'm reading, "In Search of Ancient Ireland," the writers discuss the dawn of prehistory and their kings. They gave the example of Tara, which was one of the four major kingdoms in Ireland at that time. In these pagan kingdoms, mounds were built up to communicate with the darkness. The king would stand on the mound because it was the king's responsibility to communicate with darkness. It is so interesting because today's leaders are expected to do quite the same activity, but the communicating, in some respects, is finding their own darkness. And, too, they are trying to be the intermediary, if you will, to discern what is willed for the organization.

Rich: Interestingly, listening to God's voice and trying to discern the right move for the organization leads us to another unpopular concept.

Tom: Right.

Rich: As you have guessed, I'm referring to obedience. There are three degrees of obedience to God: to his commandments, to his counsels, and to his inspirations. Here we are speaking of obedience to his inspirations. As faithful servants, we not only obey his words but whatever he makes known to us in signs. We will need to test these promptings by the teaching of Scripture and the Church, but we must not miss opportunities when God is calling us to act.

Tom: And, within a Christian context and understanding, this has to be negotiated by searching out God's will. I think that when that doesn't happen, the focus is wrong, and the results are the disasters we've seen in the industry in the last few years.

Rich: Maybe this is a great warning to those who recruit leaders. Those hiring need to be very intentional about who it is they call to their organization. Maybe it means setting aside the resumes of the candidates' accomplishments and discovering what really lives inside their souls. As a religious friar once said, "Do you want to know where God is? Where you are not."[5] In other words, God's work is where there is no self-interest. That's the kind of person who will seek the hidden voice and strive for justice in the workplace.

Journal Exercise

The Hidden Voice

The hidden voice will be heard if we prepare for it. Consider these steps:

1. Meditation
   Give the mind time to reflect. Engage yourself in a spiritual resource for personal and theological reflection.
2. Petition
   Respond to the hidden voice. Allow your thoughts to move toward God with specific intention.
3. Contemplation
   Enter into the place of intimacy with God. It is a here that we spend time with God for the sole reason of being with him. Here there are no words.
4. Action
   Strive to live out a relationship with God and act in such a way that the hidden voice influences your decisions as a leader.

Spiritual Application

Silence

Silence is hidden deep within a person. Only when that person communicates a meaning first thought of in silence is this revealed to the hearer.[6] Words have power when born of a silence that has a deep well. Silence gives birth to thought; it is the garden of reflection. Without it, we cannot listen to the hidden voice.

Silence grows out of discipline. Vibrant and full of life, silence is a great mystery—it is a returning to oneself, to that inner reserve. It is a knowing, a feeling, a living stillness, a vibrating within itself.[7] "To be capable of silence is a virtue."[8] It is as necessary to the development of character as inhaling is to the breathing cycle. Those who cannot be silent are like those who exhale only, never breathing in.

Breathing in fills the lungs, and, in the same way, silence fills the soul. The presence of God and the hidden voice are found in silence. Silence paves the way for anyone to have a genuine encounter with God. As leaders, we must cultivate silence in our lives if we are to be relevant. Some practice of meditation and reflection is necessary if we are to be sustained by someone beyond ourselves. "We seldom find God in a hurry."[9] It is said that "hurry was not of the Devil; it is the Devil."[10] Silence nurtures the image of God in us and teaches us to be still and seek the truth.

> Some practice of meditation and reflection is necessary if we are to be sustained by someone beyond ourselves.

Daily Practice

Listen to God today.

Allow silence to speak to your current circumstances. Nurture your ability to trust in God's desire to assist you. Seek to align your efforts with God's will.

How can you accomplish your work with God's help? Ask specifically for his involvement and seek to recognize him in specific events.

"Ask, and it will be given to you, seek, and you will find; knock and the door will be opened to you" (Matt. 7:7–8).

Chapter Eleven

The Other
Side

Leadership Challenge

The debate lasted for hours. The leadership team was almost equally divided on the matter. The CEO listened attentively to each contributor. He had come to the meeting with his own view of the topic of discussion. It troubled him that so many of his intimate teammates disagreed with his suggested course of action.

At first, he was annoyed that there was no clear consensus for his position. He felt as though the group was beginning to waste valuable time. His chief financial officer supported a point of view that benefited the bottom line. The chief human resource officer made a clear case for the harm the opposite decision would have upon the corporate culture. The CEO began to feel torn between loyal colleagues on both sides.

The CEO decided not to make a quick decision. He tabled the discussion for the leadership team's meeting later that same week. He asked the group to work toward a consensus, regardless of the solution, as long as it was right for the organization. The leadership team was shocked. It was obvious to everyone that the CEO was beginning to think and work differently.

How does a leader honor those who lean strongly one way or the other about an issue under discussion? How can a team begin to have influence, where all members believe that they can bring their voice to the table?

The Other Side

When a nation gives birth to a man who is able to produce thought, another is born who is able to understand and admire it.
—*Joseph Joubert*[1]

A leader's effort to listen to advisors is one of the most important marks of effective leadership. Listening will always be a prerequisite for respect and trust. Therefore, a leader must be willing to listen and discern before any major decision. Receiving input from colleagues will make leaders vulnerable to many competing voices but will also open them up to the collective intelligence within their ranks. Leaders must learn to listen for the distinctive voice of wisdom through the maze.

When is it important to act quickly, not to lose the moment, and when is it important to reflect and adhere to caution? Leaders must be able to discern when perseverance will win the day and when it is time to move quickly. They must also recognize when many hands will make light work and when there are too many cooks in the kitchen.

Furthermore, leaders must be willing to listen to points of view that they do not hold to personally. In listening we learn, in listening we yield, in listening we grow, in listening we also come to grips with what we don't know. In order for a leadership team to truly live out its mission, it must be able to influence the leader. Leaders who ignore the collective wisdom of the team create a myth about their management. If team members, advisors, and managers have no influence, then the leader perpetuates a farce to the organization that an actual leadership team exists.

On the other hand, leaders must learn when to make an executive decision, especially when a decision is required on the spot. Even under such circumstances, the discipline of listening to others as standard practice in one's life informs the decision that the leader must make in isolation.

Leaders lead only in so far as they are followed. People will follow a leader they believe in. They learn to believe in those who will listen. They learn to believe in those who respect them. They learn to believe in those who make room for them at the table of decision making. They learn to believe in the leader who recognizes there is another side and is willing to listen to it.

Years ago, the *Pryor Report* discussed how easily some conversations and proposals can be squelched simply by citing aphorisms or proverbs to make a point.[2] For example, someone supports a contrary opinion by saying, "You can't teach an old dog new tricks." The other side of the argument is, of course, "It's never too late to learn." Leaders must always be open to the other side and never miss the opportunity to reflect upon the antithesis of an idea.

All ideas need to be pondered. We become convinced by certain truths when we become acquainted with them. Knowing what we should do in certain situations is the result of years of training in listening, thinking, discussing, and challenging others and ourselves. We very often refuse to devote thought to ideas which at first appear to be rather fantastic or contrary to everything we believed. The fact that an idea is contrary to what was

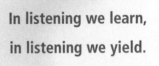

In listening we learn, in listening we yield.

believed until now is not sufficient reason to avoid considering it. It is rather noteworthy that St. Thomas Aquinas held the geocentric theory of the universe yet conceded another possibility based on a hypothesis of physics.[3]

As leaders, we must also listen to the ideas others have about us. We can learn from others if we truly want to make progress in our personal and professional lives. Undesirable qualities will impede our relationships and our work. We suggest that leaders make inquiries of trusted colleagues to explore avenues for growth. A good 360-degree feedback tool that many organizations use may also be helpful in this area. Our blind spot is often larger than we think.[4] The ability to confront colleagues at the leadership level will help define the way we work and signal our openness to self-improvement. This includes not insisting on our own rights and our need to be right.

The concept of the other side reveals something about our flexibility and openness as leaders, but even more it conveys to others something about our self-awareness. Living an aware life means that we directly face the crisis of reality.[5] We will be grounded leaders, facing the truth about ourselves and our circumstances. Bob Wicks sees self-awareness as a requirement for survival. He says, "By avoiding self-awareness we risk more than the failure to discern some possibly helpful knowledge . . . we risk losing everything!"[6] We have noticed that an organization's internal culture often reflects the leader's sense of self. If the leader is an egoist, greedy for success, mad with ambition, dominated by unruly pride, and not open to personal faults, the organization is in trouble.

> **Living an aware life means that we directly face the crisis of reality.**

The other side leaders are humble enough to know that all the answers do not reside in them. Their hidden strength is demonstrated in their ability to be challenged without being diminished. They see the possibilities in the ideas of others and welcome learning something new. They are not fooled by aphorisms or proverbs that can defend virtually any position. The other side leader is a thinking and a discerning leader—a wise leader who considers all sides but always seeks to find the truth.

The next time someone urges moving quickly on an issue (he who hesitates is lost), remind that person it might be good to look before you leap! As a leader, teach your colleagues to ponder the other side.

Fireside Chat

Tom: We've discussed that with every great leader one finds a team of people. That team is a group of people who can act as a sounding board and a means for the leader to play out decisions. Can you comment on that? I am also intrigued about truth. What is truth?

Rich: An ancient question—asked long ago. I really have observed over my professional career how difficult it is for people in leadership to be influenced by others, how difficult it is for a leader to change his or her mind once it is made up. You used an interesting term. I do think leaders are fairly good at utilizing the people around them as sounding boards. However, when you are a person who is perceived to be in authority, and a person who has a certain amount of expertise, it is really difficult to be open to hear, at times, the most unsuspecting voices coming from the most unsuspecting places. The ability to receive truth from unexpected sources is a great grace. I think this is an important chapter because leaders are supposed to know the answers. We're supposed to have the jump on everyone else. And so, there's a caution here to not only be open to learn but also willing to change.

Truth is profound. It comes from above and is proper to God alone. This is why we based our leadership philosophy on a spiritual model. Once truth is embraced, however, it must be nurtured.

Tom, what type of person are you willing to open yourself up to? With what kind of person are you able to step back and say, *I'm willing to examine what I've heard from this person and consider what I think about this issue.* What is it about that person that gives you an openness to learn from him?

Tom: I think that the greatest challenge is to find people who are willing, in a life-giving way, to not always agree with you, which happens so rarely in leadership. Leaders often have yes men surrounding them. However, those who are willing to challenge you in good faith, not antagonistically, but saying, "Have you considered?"—they are people of enormous value to you personally. I don't know if it is a flaw or a strength about my personality that I am trusting of people until they take away that trust. Many leaders say that this has to be earned. But I've discovered that if you find people who are trustworthy, in humility you can turn to them. Another principle that I hold is to use more than one muse, if you will. An organization can get lopsided if you only have one person as your sounding board. Rather, test out ideas with a group of trusted advisors. You get the breadth and depth of the knowledge of the group, and it helps you not to isolate yourself or to isolate that trusted advisor because people may come to resent him or her. So, it's really only fair to the leader and to his or her muse to choose a group of advisors. However, I would not take council with dozens of people either. I think that is dangerous. You need a small group of spiritual friends surrounding you and partnering with you because then everyone aspires to the greatest good, which is the organizational mission—not your own personal one.

> The ability to receive truth from unexpected sources is a great grace.

Rich: How difficult is it for you to receive from somebody whom you respect what you don't want to hear?

Tom: Well, I'm practiced at it now because I've heard more than I like. In my profession, where situations are coming at you one hundred miles per hour, sometimes you make decisions almost too rapidly or impetuously because that's what you feel the situation calls for. I have learned, with maturity, that I must slow down that process. Speed is really the enemy of good, and at times you need to step back, rest in the Lord, and listen to your trusted advisors. It's never easy. Sometimes you get a little resentful. But if you can take yourself out of it and realize it is not about you but about a decision or thought that you are having, then I think it is a lot easier to accept.

Rich: I want to make a suggestion to anybody who might be reading along. When the criticism is about you, I would urge you to step back and, before responding, ask yourself the question, *Could this be true of me?* That question itself may have more value than the criticism because it shows that you're willing and open to consider something that isn't comfortable. It isn't what we normally want to do.

Tom: That's difficult because leading complex, large organizations often takes a tremendous amount of ego, and to really humble yourself and make yourself vulnerable usually contradicts that ego. But I think that your point is accurate. I have one final question, and then you can make any other comments. You've been so often in an advisory role not only because of your leadership capability but also due to your background in theology, spirituality, and therapy. How do you manage to take such a message to a CEO, and how do you phrase it in a way that he or she can hear it?

Rich: I try to do it in the context of relationship building. Part of it is accepting this role as my calling or vocation. That makes it a lot easier. Fortunately, I have advised people who have worked in depth on their personal development and spirituality, which always helps. Personally, I find it is easier to say something difficult to someone I really love or care about because I am doing it not only on the virtue of charity, but also a personal posture of love that seeks that person's highest good. The intention and motivation behind one's challenge is fundamental. Another consideration is that those who wish to grow in truth and in the love of God must wage constant war against self-love. As a messenger, I must be willing to live by the message as well. This, in my better moments, has allowed me to say what I needed to say without being arrogant and haughty.

Journal Exercise

The Other Side

Reflect on the material below and contemplate that there is always another side.[7]

Wise Old Sayings and Their Antitheses

1. *You can't teach an old dog new tricks. vs. It's never too late to learn.*
2. *Look before you leap. vs. He who hesitates is lost.*
3. *Out of sight, out of mind. vs. Absence makes the heart grow fonder.*
4. *Two heads are better than one. vs. If you want something done right, do it yourself.*
5. *Never look a gift horse in the mouth. vs. All that glitters is not gold.*
6. *Better safe than sorry. vs. Nothing ventured, nothing gained.*

Spiritual Application

Docility

Seeing the other side requires that we are ready and willing to be taught by (docile) and yielded, when appropriate, to another's direction. Being docile and teachable is part of the virtue of prudence. A leader must have humility to be docile and must be prudent enough to seek good counsel.

Since we are not our own but belong to God, there are duties we must address—duties to God and to each other. We cannot, therefore, simply do with our own lives what we want. We must also be willing to learn about a life of stewardship, which recognizes that we are not the owners of our lives, our talents, and our treasures but stewards entrusted to manage another's property.[8] This simple fact presumes obedience to God and accountability to our neighbor. Leaders must recognize the inevitable conflict, for themselves and others, between the gratification of human passion and these duties.

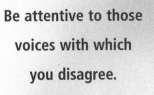

Be attentive to those voices with which you disagree.

A teachable personality is the hallmark of a virtuous life, and docility is the necessary virtue for any developmental path. To lead and influence others, we must keep learning. This investment in ourselves has been called the principle of preparation.[9] This principle states that results improve to the extent that leaders develop themselves and their followers. When we understand who we are and why we are here, our desire to become what we were meant to be is the natural fruit of one's life; we say then "Teach me, O Lord, Thy ways."

Daily Practice

Be attentive to those voices with which you disagree. Ask yourself why you disagree. Challenge your thinking with several results in mind:

- What can I learn from that with which I disagree? Is there any merit to the reasoning behind this voice?
- How can I gain greater clarity and conviction through this challenge?
- When would it be appropriate to change my own views? Why?

Chapter Twelve

The Mystery of Longing

Leadership Challenge

Rebecca was in her twenty-second year of health-care leadership, ten of those as a chief executive officer. This was her most difficult year. She felt isolated and lonely. Difficult decisions led to the termination of a leader colleague as well as to the resignation of a long-term colleague/friend.

At the age of forty-six, Rebecca had never married, but the thought of marriage and a solid relationship was on her mind. Her career had always been her priority. She was respected in the community and in the workplace. Many of the men she felt attracted to over the years were men of character and values, but so often they were in her own organization. She knew the danger of mixing business and pleasure in this environment. She never wanted to be accused of having a conflict of interests.

Rebecca surrounded herself with good people. She understood the adage, however, "it's lonely at the top." She spent a lot of time considering the weight of leadership and wanted time to contemplate the problem from afar.

Lately Rebecca longed for human contact to meet both a personal and social need. She found herself seeking God's guidance about her career and determined that if the right person came along, she would make some career sacrifices, if necessary.

How should Rebecca pay attention to her loneliness? What career options does an executive like Rebecca have?

The Mystery of Longing

Often, the call to leadership is a call to loneliness. In the life of every leader there is the triumphant entry into Jerusalem but also the reality of Gethsemane. It is in the darkness of the Garden of Gethsemane that the leader explores the most important reality—a relationship with God.

As a youth, the lure of leadership seems compelling and desirable—status, wealth, and power beyond all imagination. However, business schools fail to tell students about the profound loneliness that leading people in organizations can bring. There is a deep longing to be understood and a great desire to be connected with others. Let's search the mystery of this longing and try to identify the great gift that is leadership.

One need only look at a photograph of Abraham Lincoln when he was elected president and reflect on a similar image four years later, in 1864, to recognize the heavy burden that leadership carries. At a time when it would have been easier to allow the rhythm of history to deal with the issue of slavery and when it would have been easier to allow the current in the country to pull it apart, one man had a vision of unity and of the greatness of America. In some respects, the Union was preserved through the blood of America's citizens and the absolute iron will of its leader who, in the end, gave his own blood, too. There can be no doubt that as one reflects on the history of that era, Lincoln's call to leadership was as profoundly lonely and bereft of honor and glory as any could be.

At the advent of World War II, one leader alone, Winston Churchill, stood triumphantly before the overarching power of evil emanating from Nazi Germany as other powers fell rapidly in the tornado of Western Europe. And yet for every leader's triumph there may be a Waterloo; there may also be an island, like Elba, of loneliness.

When a person assumes a leadership position, that leader accepts the responsibility, not only for the organization, but for the hopes and aspirations of its people, the expectation of its community of support and its customers, and the burden of the anticipations of an outside world, which is often hostile.

In this burden of responsibility the leader feels connected to the entirety of his or her organization but often finds a lack of connectedness with others. The expectations and anticipation of how a leader should act creates an abyss that is sometimes difficult to traverse. A leader often strives to be understood. It may come as a complete surprise to others that the leader also longs to be understood and known. A leader would prefer to be liked, though this is not the expectation. Anyone who has been a leader knows that it is impossible to please everyone. If a leader walks through a department and fails to smile on a certain day, a staff member will accuse that leader of all sorts of hidden agendas and burdens. Yet, if the staffer didn't smile, he or she would say that he or she was having a bad day and shouldn't have to smile at the leader anyway.

> It may come as a complete surprise to others that the leader also longs to be understood and known.

Most leaders will tell you that they would love to be free from the burden of responsibility, and despite the allure of money and power, the sacrifices have often been too much. What can we discern from this great mystery of longing? What can we do to protect ourselves from this overarching burden of loneliness? First and foremost, leadership has everything to do with the people with whom we surround ourselves. We need to be surrounded by people who care for and nurture us, who ask the questions, and who protect us in those moments of agony, not as much from the outside world as from ourselves and the sometimes deep desire to run.

Re-reading chapter 9 with some frequency will be of great value. Staying on track with this theme will not always be easy. We have, in the example of Christ, a group of disciples, friends who followed him, supported him, prayed with him, ate with him, listened to him, questioned him, celebrated with him, and wept with him. Leaders are known by the people closest to them, whether they are people of principle and, more important, if they can help sustain a vision when it is imperiled by the dark, deep agony and pain that leadership can sometimes bring.

They must be people of principle. Abraham Lincoln said, "men of principle are the principal men." Here, then, is the true test of a leader, to surround one's self with competent and close allies, to be in relationship with people whose trust is authentic, whose support is real, and whose courage is sustaining. As Rilke said, "I want to be with those who know secret things, or else alone."[1]

The other great mystery of this darkness of leadership is that leadership is a calling. Why would God ever call a person to such loneliness and heartbreak? Of course, the answer is God would not; if he has placed a leader in the position of stewardship, the leader is a person near and dear to God's heart. The leader who responds confidently with a "yes" to God can be assured that, although the path of leadership will never cease to be a challenge, God, in his providence, will provide the moral courage, the virtue, and his love to sustain that leader no matter how dark the hour.

> He will lead us to the one true companion of this lonely journey—himself.

However, we should not expect that the rewards will be in this world. In our "yes" to God to accept the mantle of leadership as stewards of his people or his goods or his services, we make a contract with him and have an understanding. That understanding is that our rewards may be heavenly, yet our confidence is that God has put us here for a purpose and that we, with Ignatius, ask him to use us for his good. God's covenant to us is that he will give us the graces that we need to live out our calling in the character of a leader, and he will lead us to the one true companion of this lonely journey—himself.

As we ponder our solitude and draw deeply from the well there, we can find the one hidden voice that is within us—the voice of God. We must always be in a prayerful stance in order to continually reassess ourselves before our God—and we must humbly become vulnerable before him. As we do, that one distinct voice, the one above all the other voices in our lives, will be made clear, and the path, no matter how difficult it may be, will be evident.

Fireside Chat

Rich: I'm going to begin with some comments and maybe they will lead to a question. We're at the end of our  time together with the fireside chats. In essence, we are putting the finishing touches on our book. Reading and reflecting on this chapter about the mystery of longing has provoked some stirrings and feelings within me. When we discuss the mystery of longing, there is something inside of me that recognizes that mystery even today. I have many feelings about the years that I have led people, about all the time that I was entrusted with responsibility and was a part of organizations. I am longing especially to comprehend more deeply the mystery of servanthood. I am now trying to understand this strong desire within me to be a servant, to want to lead less and follow more. Maybe this takes us back not only to our roots but to the question of where leadership begins. And that is, in order to be a great leader, do you, to some degree, have to be a good follower?

Tom: I think you're right, Rich. I really like the quote by Rilke that we used in the chapter: "I want to be with those who know secret things, or else alone." I think those secrets are actually sort of the mystery, the profound mystery, that every human being has to go home to God. We have just an incredible example of leadership through the humility of the cross. Here, the leader of all humanity humbles himself as a servant and dies an ignominious death on the cross. Relying on the action of God's power, Jesus is the King of the entire world through that unselfish offering. That, to me, is the model of servant leadership. To really be the leader, we must not only humble ourselves but also be broken and at times be lonely. There is probably nothing lonelier than the cross, yet after the cross comes the most profound incident of all creation. That is the resurrection of the Savior. In that moment of God's holy and most marvelous work (I believe Augustine said that), we have what servant leadership is all about. And so, Rich, what we have talked about is a journey that starts with loneliness and has its highs and its lows. In the end is the profound joy of the relationship we have with God. Everybody else along the way, even those people that have shared our secrets, are really helping point the way. Part of our mission is to help point the way for other people. That's why a leader only wants wholesome, good, spiritual relationships. I think that we as servant-leaders have to see that and learn as quickly as we can.

> These consolations are deeply personal between God and you.

Rich: In light of the redemption, the mystery of longing is related to our attempt to understand how to be for an organization what Christ was for the world. The leadership model that he exemplified is not a popular one nor an easy one, given the expectations that are placed upon us. Yet we long to follow in the footsteps of Christ. We long to be sacrificial leaders. We

long to humble ourselves. We long to be servants.
The Lord himself asks this of us when he says, "Be ye
holy, because I, the Lord your God, am holy" (Lev.
19:2). In the spiritual movement, we, as Christians,
must travel from ourselves to God and will never reach
God if we do not first depart from ourselves. This
involves a movement away from sin and the comfort of
the world (including popularity). This transformation is
effected principally by the grace of God—but it is
lonely, precisely because it is the road less traveled.

Tom: Yes. Scripture indicates that to engage in that mystery
there is a Gethsemane and there is a way to the cross.
That's hard for us, and even
though we want to be
servant-leaders, the reality
is that the path is narrow
and the way is long. And I
think it is frightening. I
think in the midst of this
loneliness and this desire to
really fully participate in
that mystery is a profound
sense of spirituality and the
need to pray. We must be constantly prayerful and
daily prayerful. We need to be minute-by-minute
seeking God about what we do. When leaders are
not that connected with God, they lose their way, and
it is then that organizations lose theirs.

> There is a plan for our lives and that life has meaning for us personally.

Rich: Maybe we could end with summing up the mystery
in another way. You know that you're being faithful
when, despite all of the difficulties, spiritual consolations come your way. These consolations are deeply
personal between God and you. They are, however,
what sustains the leader who leads from within, and
over time, never fail to produce fruit. As Saint
Gregory says, the love of God is never idle, but it
works great things.

Journal Exercise
The Mystery of Longing

Examine your role as a leader. Listen to your longings.

- Where do you experience greatest satisfaction?
- What dreams are you leaving unfulfilled?
- What do you wish was different about your life?
- What would be the result of sharing your longings with God?

Talk through these questions with a mentor, trusted friend, or spiritual director. See if any changes are in store for you.

Spiritual Application
Grace

Amazing grace how sweet the sound
that saved a wretch like me
I once was lost but now I'm found
was blind but now I see.[2]

What exactly is grace, and why is it relevant for you and me? Grace reforms our nature, restores the image of God to our souls, and makes us pleasing in the sight of God.[3] Grace strengthens us and makes us whole. It fills the void of loneliness. It is the most wonderful gift from the most wonderful kind of lover; a lover who makes Himself available to us. "Grace is God's turning himself toward us, not just to display himself as in a drama, but to grant a share in himself."[4]

Can you allow grace to speak to your current circumstances, including the loneliness of leadership, knowing that at the heart of the universe you are loved with an infinite love—a love that wills your best and seeks only your cooperation? Grace helps us understand we are not self-sufficient. We are in need of assistance on our journey.

Grace is a gift from God. It comes to us in very practical ways and reminds us that we are not alone—that we are loved—that there is a plan for our lives and that life has meaning for us personally.

Daily Practice

The mystery of longing is different for each one of us. Allow grace to sustain you in the darkest moments and strengthen you in moments of vulnerability. Each day accept the embrace of such a wonderful gift as grace.

> *The Lord has promised good to me,*
> *his word my hope secures;*
> *he will my shield and portion be,*
> *as long as life endures.*[5]

Conclusion

*It is the spirit of a person
that hangs above him
like a star in the sky.
People identify with him
until there is formed
a parade of men and women,
thus inspired.*

GEORGE MATTHEW ADAMS[1]

Conclusion

A journey has ended. You have taken the time to reflect upon leadership concepts and personal growth. Strive now to persevere in living out your calling as a leader in relationship to the topics discussed.

We, the authors, write and lead with the firm conviction that God wants to guide and teach willing travelers. Determined that we will not be whole until we have wrestled fully with the challenge laid before us as leaders, we contend that making our way through all of this will require a very specific course: Enter into the chamber and lift the veil. God will help you see him face to face.

Notes

Chapter 1

1. The Reverend James D. Watkins, comp., *Manual of Prayers* (Rome, It.: Pontifical North American College, 1996), 260.
2. Francis J. Ripley, *This Is the Faith* (Rockford, Ill.: Tan Books and Publishing, Inc., 2002), 9.
3. Ibid., 9–10.
4. Ibid., 12.
5. William Shakespeare, *Collected Works* (Kansas City, Mo.: Angelus Press), 35.
6. Saint Augustine, *The Confessions of St. Augustine,* trans. Edward B. Pusey (New York: Washington Square Press, Inc., 1961), 1.
7. Ripley, *This Is the Faith,* 7.
8. Richard Glenn, "Moving Toward Transformational Leadership," (St. Louis, Mo.: *Health Progress*, 1998), 63.
9. Ibid., 64.
10. Fr. B. W. Maturin, *Self-Knowledge and Self-Discipline* (1915; reprint, Harrison, N.Y.: Roman Catholic Books, n.d.), 11.
11. Rudolf Allers, *Self Improvement* (London: Burns and Washbourne, 1939; reprint Fort Collins, Colo.: Roman Catholic Books, 2000), 23. Citations are to the Roman Catholic Books edition.

Chapter 2

1. Donald DeMarco, *The Many Faces of Virtue* (Steubenville, Ohio: Emmaus Road Publishing, 2000), 54.
2. B. C. Forbes, *Thoughts on Leadership* (Chicago: Triumph Books, 1995), 140.
3. Ibid., 139.
4. Ella Wheeler Wilcox "The Winds of Fate" *World Voices* (New York: Hearst's International Library Company, 916). n.p.
5. Romano Guardini, *Learning the Virtues* (Manchester, N.H.: Sophia Institute Press, 1998), 4.
6. Ibid., 22.
7. Demarco, 54.
8. Ripley, *This Is the Faith,* 7.
9. Ibid., 36.

Chapter 3

1. Jeffrey J. Fox, *How to Become CEO* (New York: Hyperion, 1998), 55.
2. Forbes, 99.
3. Ibid., 144.
4. Robert Fritz, *The Path of Least Resistance* (New York: Fawcett Columbine Books, 1989), 172.
5. Glenn, "Transformational Leadership," 63–64.
6. Ibid.
7. Jim Collins, *Good to Great* (New York: Harper Collins Publishing, Inc., 2001), 21.

8. Margaret J. Wheatley, *Leadership and the New Science* (San Francisco, Calif.: Berrett-Koehler Publishers, Inc., 1994), 144.

9. Ibid.

10. Forbes, 101.

11. Daniel Goleman, *Working with Emotional Intelligence* (New York: Bantam Books, 1998), 32.

12. Forbes, 38.

13. Ibid., 37.

Chapter 4

1. Carol Robinson, *My Life with Thomas Aquinas* (Kansas City, Mo.: Angelus Press, 1995), 35.

2. Richard Glenn, *Transform: Twelve Tools for Life* (Franklin, Tenn.: Providence House Publishers, 2003), 9.

3. "The Picture of Dorian Gray." Dorian Gray was a character in an Oscar Wilde story who never aged, always showing a perfect face to the world. But hidden away in his attic was a hideous portrait of him that showed every sin, flaw, and disgusting act. It aged and showed the true character of the man.

4. Fr. John Laux, *Catholic Morality* (Rockford, Ill.: Tan Books and Publishers, Inc., 1990), 28.

5. Ibid., 29.

6. Leon J. Supernaut Jr., "Morality is Habit Forming" *The Publication of Catholics United for the Faith* (April 2001): 28.

7. C. S. Lewis, *The Abolition of Man* (New York: Macmillan Press, 1943), 87–88.

Chapter 5

1. Glenn, *Transform,* 84.

2. Goleman, 26–27.

3. Chip Dodd, *The Voice of the Heart* (Franklin, Tenn.: Providence House Publishers, 2001); see cover subtitle: *A Call to Full Living.*

4. Ibid., 4.

5. Glenn, *Transform,* see chapter 10 on the Holistic Model.

6. Ibid., 84.

7. C. S. Lewis, *The Joyful Christian* (New York: Macmillan Publishing Company, Inc., 1977), 30.

Chapter 6

1. George Leo Haydock, *The Douay-Rheims New Testament with a Catholic Commentary* (Monrovia, Calif.: Catholic Treasures, 1991), 1258.

2. Dorothy Sayers, *Creed or Chaos* (Sophia Institute Press: Manchester, N.H.: 1974), 63.

3. James Allen, *As a Man Thinketh* (Fort Worth, Tex.: Brownlow Publishing Company, Inc., 1985), 11.

4. Robinson, 174.

5. Ibid., 256.

6. Allen, 18.

Notes

7. Bob Wicks, *Riding the Dragon* (Notre Dame, Ind.: Sorin Books, 2003), 110.
8. Allen, 49.
9. Forbes, 12.

Chapter 7

1. Forbes, 136.
2. Ripley, *This Is the Faith*, 6.
3. Ibid., 6–7.
4. The Congregation of the Mission, "Questions & Answers: What Are the Key Elements of Vincentian Discernment?" http://vincentians.net/newsite/faqs.php?mode=view&faqCat=Discernment.
5. Burt Nanus, *The Leader's Edge* (Chicago: Contemporary Books, 1989), 101.
6. David Cottrell, *Listen Up Leader* (Dallas, Tex.: Cornerstone Leadership Institute, 2000), 30–32.
7. Peter Kreeft, *Back to Virtue* (San Francisco, Calif.: Ignatius Press, 1986), 74.
8. Romano Guardini, *Learning the Virtues* (Manchester, N.H.: Sophia Institute Press, 1998), 4.
9. Ibid., 9.
10. Ibid.
11. Kreeft, 74.
12. Venerable Louis of Granada, O.P., *Summa of the Christian Life, vol. 2*, trans. and adapt. Fr. Jordan Aumann, O.P. (Rockford, Ill.: Tan Books and Publishers, Inc., 1979), 86.

Chapter 8

1. Robinson, 35.
2. Robert J. Wicks, *Availability: The Problem and the Gift* (New York: Paulist Press, 1986), 25.
3. Ibid., 27.
4. Ibid., 29.
5. Glenn, *Transform*, 84.
6. United States Catholic Conference, *Catechism of the Catholic Church*, (Washington, D.C.: United States Catholic Conference, Inc.—Libreria Editrice Vaticana 1994), no. 1806.

Chapter 9

1. Venerable Louis of Granada, 5.
2. Ibid., 8
3. Edwin Faust, "Friendly Advice from Aelred," *The Latin Mass: A Journal of Catholic Culture* (fall 2003): 27.
4. Ibid., 26, 28.
5. Ibid., 30.
6. Venerable Louis of Granada, 181.
7. Faust, 27.
8. Faust, 29.
9. DeMarco, 161.
10. Faust, 30.

Chapter 10
1. Dante Alighieri, *The Divine Comedy.* canto 1, line 1–3.
2. Théophile Desbonnets, *Assisi, Steps of a Saint: A Spiritual Guide* (Paris, 1971), 101.
3. Venerable Louis of Granada, 27.
4. Ibid., 64.
5. Ibid., 348.
6. Guardini, 175.
7. Ibid., 176.
8. Ibid.
9. Morton T. Kelsey, *The Other Side of Silence* (New York: Paulist Press,1976), 83.
10. Ibid.

Chapter 11
1. Forbes, 90.
2. "Practical Ideas for Managing People . . . And Yourself," *The Pryor Report* (February 1993): 12.
3. Allers, *Self Improvement*, 217.
4. Glenn, *Transform*, 20.
5. Wicks, 20.
6. Ibid.
7. "Practical Ideas," 12.
8. Glenn, *Transform*, 69–70.
9. David Cottrell, *Monday Morning Leadership* (Dallas, Tex.: Cornerstone Leadership Institute, 2002), 103.

Chapter 12
1. David Whyte, *The Heart Aroused,* quoting a poem by Rainer Maria Rilke, trans. Robert Bly (New York: Doubleday, 1994), 138.
2. Newton, John, 1725–1807, "Amazing Grace."
3. Venerable Louis of Granada, 64.
4. Medard Kehl and Werner Loser, eds., *The von Balthasar Reader* (New York: Crossword Publishing Co., 1982), 337.
5. Newton, "Amazing Grace."

Conclusion
1. Forbes, 142.